Bill,
There is a f_
than a brother. ....

TAKING THE LONG
WAY HOME

Adventures of a Retired Couple
Biking Across America

G Frank Miller

G Frank Miller

Behold, how good and pleasant it is
when brothers dwell in unity. Psalm 133:1

ITB

Frank HH13

ISBN 13: 978-1478392927
ISBN 10: 1478392924

Printed by Create Space, North Charleston, SC

The author is responsible for the cover photo, all interior photos, and the maps.

DEDICATION

Many people had a hand in this story of our adventure riding bikes across North America. I've tried to mention all of them in the body of this book. However, one person is very special. I'm dedicating this book to Helen, my wife and riding partner, without whom this adventure would never have happened. She was the inspiration that motivated me to plan and execute this very long way home. In fact, my life with Helen has been a continuous adventure since we first met in 1964 in Saltillo, Mexico. While we were riding across the continent, I kept an email journey that I called *Travels with Helen*. That was the working title for this book. I changed it to *Taking the Long Way Home*. This journey ended, but I'm still traveling with Helen.

CONTENTS

PROLOGUE

My wife, Helen, and I started our retirement planning about 1990. If all the plans worked out, we should be in a position to retire in 1996. Our youngest son, Brad, should be graduating from college that year, and I'd have about 30 years of service with the Arlington Public Schools in Virginia. Arlington was a great place to live and work. It was close to Washington, D.C., but with a smaller town feeling. Raising our sons there had been good, but we decided retirement would be a time to relocate. We'd start our new life in a new place.

Helen's grandfather had bought land south of Melbourne, Florida, on the mainland shore of the Indian River Lagoon before she was born. He built a house where the family lived from time to time, and where her older brother, John, now lives. Robert, her other brother, had recently moved to Florida from Maryland. He and his wife, Judy, live nearby. When we made the decision to make Florida our retirement home, being near family was a consideration. We build our home on the barrier island across the Indian River Lagoon from her brothers. The community name, Sunnyland Beach, brought up an image of pure Florida. What could be better than starting a new life in a place named Sunnyland Beach?

The move to Florida took place in late 1996. We no longer lived nearly in the shadow of the Washington Monument, but were now making our home on the barrier island between the Atlantic Ocean and the Indian River Lagoon about five miles

5

north of Sebastian Inlet. The beach was a short walk away, and a canal to the lagoon with our own dock was just a few steps out our back door. We also had a new development with a golf course right next door.

Western Maryland College had a nine-hole golf course. As a freshman, Brad started playing with his buddies. I played a little golf while growing up in Iowa. I gave up golf after I married Helen and we started our family, but I still had my old clubs stored in our attic. Now with Brad starting to play, I thought it would be a good time to get back into golf. Helen announced she wasn't going to be left at home, and let me know she was aware women also played golf. We began playing some while in Virginia, and enjoyed playing together even though we didn't play very well.

I once heard Arnold Palmer say that golf is seductive. What he meant was no matter how bad you play, you will have a good shot during a round that will make you think you can play the game. Truth be told, no one can master this sport, but everyone thinks they might be the first. We were seduced when we got to Florida. Helen and I played a lot, almost every day, and with lessons, our scores improved. As long as I was improving, I loved to play. However, when my game plateaued toward the end of 1999, I had a hard time dealing with not improving. I even got to the point where I would slam clubs down after a bad shot, and wanted to throw them in a pond. Helen still enjoyed playing. She had a much better attitude.

Three things then happened that changed my life. The first was something I read in one of Jan Karen's Mitford series of

6

books. The main character in these books is an Episcopal priest, Father Tim. In one of the books, he has retired, and is struggling with what he should do with the rest of his life. Reading the Bible one day, he read Psalm 139:16; *your eyes saw my unformed substance, in your book were written, every one of them, the days that were formed for me, when as yet there was none of them.* Like the fictional Father Tim, I was struck by this verse. I realized that the Lord has a plan for my life, and my poor attitude toward golf was His way of telling me He had something more for my life than 18 holes of golf every day. I had been living my days like I had gotten to a blank page in the book, but I knew the Lord wouldn't have blanks in His plan for my life. It was time to discover His plan for after my career in education.

The second life-changing event started in January of 2000 when Ricci and Dee Waters came to visit us. They had been our next door neighbors in Arlington. As the children grew up, Helen and Ricci spent a lot of time sitting on the front steps talking about life, while watching the neighborhood kids play. They shared a lot of personal experiences and aspirations. Helen had expressed a desire to ride a bicycle across the country. She had mentioned this to me, but I hadn't taken her seriously.

One day during the January visit, Ricci told about a friend who was planning to ride a bicycle with her husband from Northern Virginia to Seattle, Washington. I wasn't paying a lot of attention to the conversation until I heard Ricci ask Helen if she still wanted to ride across the country. Helen replied something about wanting to do it, but she didn't think I was interested. I spoke up, and announced we would make that cross-country bike ride in 2001. They thought I was joking, but I wasn't. This might have been my Father Tim moment. It seemed like what I was supposed to do, and I wasn't sure why. The commitment to ride across North America became the primary focus of my attention for the next year and changed my life forever.

During the year of planning for the cross-country trip, we were kept very busy finding the right equipment, selecting a route, and making arrangements to be on the road for an extended period of time. I read several books and articles that helped point us in the right direction. In the November 2000 issue of *Adventure Cyclist* magazine, Willie Weir wrote: *Adventures are many, many things . . . but they are never planned. Trips are planned. Adventure is what happens when the plan takes a detour.* This trip was going to be an adventure.

As the day for our departure drew near, the third life changing event occurred. The Chapel by the Sea, the church we had become a part of in Florida, had its annual Missions Conference a couple of weeks before our departure. The speaker was John Mariner, the executive director of World Witness, the foreign missions board for the Associate Reformed Presbyterian Church. John challenged the church members to get involved in missions, and talked about some specific opportunities available to retirees.

When John issued his challenge, I leaned over to Helen and said, "We could do that." She nodded in agreement. When the

8

session ended, we walked up to him and I said, "We are interested in the program you talked about where short-term missionaries teach English in Russia."

I was astonished when Helen said, "I'm not." As my mouth dropped open, she went on to say, "I want to do something in a Spanish speaking country."

John noticed my surprise at Helen's comment and said, "I have just the thing for you. Let's have lunch tomorrow after church. I'll tell you about it."

The next day, we learned about a need for someone to implement a program to teach English to seminary students in Tampico, Mexico. This was right down Helen's alley. She had been a teacher of English to students from foreign countries, and had majored in Spanish in college. Most of my career had been in administration. Organizing a new English program was a challenge that was right up my line. We told John we had a little trip planned, and would be busy for several months. This didn't bother him. We all agreed that when we returned from our bike ride we'd make a trip to Mexico to check it out. Little did we suspect at that time how the Lord would use the bike ride as preparation for a mission work in Mexico?

Traveling with Helen has given me a wonderful opportunity for adventure. It started in 2001 with a bike ride and is still continuing.

While on the bike ride, I wrote a daily email journal of each day's ride. I titled them *Travels with Helen.* We knew our family and friends worried about us as we rode bikes across deserts, over mountains, through major cities, and over wide

9

rivers. For that reason, I wrote the emails so as not to always reveal the challenges and dangers we were facing. Now I can tell the whole story. These emails were the primary source for the stories of this adventure I have titled *Taking the Long Way Home.*

Helen is ready to go.

CHAPTER 1

GETTING TO THE STARTING LINE

The year of preparation for the bike adventure was filled with activity. For the first time since retirement, I went into my school administrator planning mode. I checked out all the books in the library on long distance bike rides. We needed to learn about equipment, routes, and training.

Talking to people in bike shops was a great resource. A bike shop operator in Cocoa Beach had just returned from a cross-continent ride. We went up to pick his brain about equipment and routes. His first question when we related what we were planning was, "How many are going?" When we told him it was just the two of us, he remarked this was the perfect number. He then told stories about his experience, and how frustrating it was to ride for such a long time with a group. There were places he wanted to stop and explore, but the group needed to keep pushing on. He felt he missed a lot. Stories like his and others were helpful as the pieces started to fall into place.

The decision to travel alone was significant. This meant we would be traveling the whole distance across the country without a support vehicle to carry our equipment. We would be on our own when we had a problem. There is no way to travel across North America and not encounter deserts and mountains. We needed to be prepared for any mechanical or physical problem that could occur miles from someone who could help us. I made lists of things we'd need to meet every possible emergency. The list got very long before reality set in. I realized everything on the list would have to be carried on our bikes. At that point the list was cut to what was essential and light weight.

The first items we needed were bikes. I didn't even own a bike when I committed to this adventure. After trying out different types, we learned that the bicycle company Trek made a model they called a touring bike. It looked like a light weight road bike, but on further examination we found that the wheels and tires were a little larger, and the geometry of the bike was different to make room for carrying the bags called panniers. These bikes had been designed for a cross country ride like ours. They were exactly what we needed. Having identical bikes, all parts were interchangeable.

After the bikes, we started accumulating the things we'd be carrying. We would each have two large panniers on racks over the rear wheels and two smaller ones on the front. I also had a handlebar bag where I could carry maps, and other things that needed to be handy while traveling. When we finally got on the road, my panniers weighed in at 50 pounds. Helen's were about 35 pounds.

My bike with all the gear I carried.

I was studying routes while we were in the process of getting equipped. My first thought was to leave from our home in Sunnyland Beach and ride west with our goal being someplace on the Northern California coast. This would take us through Sacramento where Brad was living and Davis, California, where we would see my sister, Jo, and her family.

Each state has a Bike and Pedestrian Coordinator who is responsible for identifying bike and pedestrian routes in their state. I contacted each of them, and got good info from Colorado, Florida, and Oklahoma. The info from other states was sort of helpful, but I don't think the tax payers in Utah, Texas, and Louisiana got their money's worth.

While most people travel west to east to take advantage of the prevailing west winds, leaving from home had some definite advantages. We wouldn't have to worry about transporting

13

everything west to get to the starting point. We would also be starting on more familiar roads which would keep us in our comfort zone for a few days at the beginning. I was sure we would be in such good condition by the time we left that a little head wind wouldn't be a factor.

The book titled *Roll Around Heaven All Day* by Stan Purdum was one I had checked out of the local library, and found very informative. Purdum wrote about a bike ride he took alone that closely followed the route I had identified. The big difference being he was riding it from west to east. I suggested that Helen read this book to give her a better feel for the planning we would need to be doing. When she was about half way through the book, I knew I was in trouble when I heard the book slam shut followed by her loudly saying, "Find another route or I'm not going." She had arrived at where Purdum had described becoming very sick while going over a 12,000 foot pass in Colorado. This was on my route. Helen didn't want to have to deal with altitude sickness, and I couldn't blame her. I had to find another route, or lose my traveling companion.

From my research, I knew the Adventure Cycling Association in Missoula, Montana, had identified several cross-country bike routes. One of them is what they call the Southern Tier Route from San Diego to Saint Augustine, Florida. We purchased a set of these maps and also were converted to going west to east. This would get us to the Atlantic Ocean just 150 miles north of our home. Riding a couple of days south by the ocean on highway A1A sounded like a good way to conclude

14

our adventure. We committed to that route and set April 1, 2001, as the starting date.

Once we had our bikes, we could start our training. Helen is the type of person who loves to exercise because she knows it is good for her. I, on the other hand, tend to exercise because I want to be in condition to do something physical like climbing a mountain, or riding a bike across the continent. My mentality is to exercise to get in shape for *the big game*. Preparing for the 2001 ride was motivation for both of us. The best way to get ready was to log a lot of miles on the bikes.

Our daily training ride was to pedal from home out to A1A, turn either north or south, and start riding. The only thing close to a hill out on the barrier island is the bridge over Sebastian Inlet. We also could go north to the Melbourne Causeway to get in a little extra hill experience. The wind was like a hill when it was in our face, and the wind blows a lot at the beach.

Often we put our loaded panniers on the bikes to make our training more realistic. It was interesting that with the panniers we didn't really feel a lot of difference. They lowered the center of gravity which made the bikes ride even steadier.

In early December, we decided it was time to give the loaded bikes a multiple day test ride. Helen's brother, Robert, and his wife, Judy, live over on the mainland. They had been along on some of our training rides. The plan was for us to ride from our home over to theirs, and spend the night. We would have our panniers loaded for this training exercise.

When the day for our test ride arrived, we rode north crossing over the Melbourne Causeway on our way to their house. Coming back the next day, we went south from Robert's and Judy's, crossing over to the island on the Wabasso Causeway. Robert and Judy rode with us on the return home until just north of the town of Sebastian. They then turned back while Helen and I continued down to Wabasso, and crossing over to the island.

We got to A1A on the island side of the Wabasso Causeway and turned north for home. After a few miles we stopped at a beachside park to refill water bottles and rest. I was in the lead as we left the park. When I got out to the highway, I noticed Helen wasn't following. Riding back into the park, I found her lying on the ground under her bike. She had lost her balance while trying to turn her bike in a tight place, and fell, hitting her elbow on the sidewalk. Immediately she knew she was injured. We were still ten miles from home, and Helen couldn't ride her bike. We decided I'd ride home, get the car, and come back for Helen and her bike.

About an hour later, when I got back to the park with the car, it was obvious that Helen's elbow was badly injured. She was experiencing a lot of pain. An ice pack wasn't going to be enough first aid. We went straight down to the hospital in Vero Beach where X-rays showed she had broken a bone. Her arm was immobilized, and she was ordered to stay off her bike until the later part of February. This put a real damper on her training. After agonizing over changing our plans, we decided to stick with our departure date. Helen is a real warrior. It takes more than a broken elbow to stop her.

On the 16th of March, we took our bikes to Alan's Bike Shop in Vero Beach. At that time, our training rides had put about 3000 miles on each bike. They felt like old friends. Libby Harrow at Alan's had been a big help as we prepared for this ride. We had arranged for her to box up our bikes, and send them to a shop in San Diego. Lord willing, they would be reassembled, and waiting for us on March 30.

Sending off the bikes was a little like sending our child to camp. The receiving bike shop had been recommended by a bike club in San Diego. We didn't know anything about this shop, or the club for that matter. We had to go on faith they were as reliable as we had been told. Our hope was the bikes would be waiting for us when we went to pick them up. In the back of my mind, I feared the bike shop would have them on display, and one of their eager sales people would sell them before we arrived.

After sending off the bikes, Helen and I flew to Sacramento where we spent some time with Brad, and Jo and Bill Retzer. Finally, March 30 came, and Brad flew with us to San Diego. What a great feeling of relief we had when we found the bike shop, and there were our bikes waiting for us. The next day we would start our adventure.

At dawn on March 31, we were with Brad at what was the starting point for our bike ride across North America. However, our backs were not against the Pacific Ocean. In fact, we were at almost 4000 feet above sea level.

The week before, while with the Retzers (my sister, Jo, and her husband, Bill, and daughter, Kate), in Davis, Helen had

17

expressed concern about being able to even make it out of San Diego since she had missed so much training time with her broken elbow. This first step of the long trip was one of the most challenging on our entire route. It would take us from sea level at Spanish Landing on the San Diego water front to almost 4000 feet at Tecate Divide. Helen was anxious about being able to make this climb. She was on the verge of backing out. She had only been riding for two weeks before we had to ship the bikes.

Everyone was trying to encourage her. Each of us knew she had a reason to be concerned. All of our ideas were pretty lame until Bill asked why we couldn't do that section in reverse? Riding from Tecate Divide to San Diego involves some climbing, but it would be more downhill than uphill. No one thought it would be cheating.

As the sun rose in the east on March 31, 2001, Brad took a photo of us looking east as we actually prepared to ride west from Tecate Divide to San Diego. We said a prayer, and our adventure started as I followed Helen down the road to San Diego.

The starting point for the Southern Tier Route

At Tecate Divide

CHAPTER 2

CALIFORNIA
March 31 to April 5

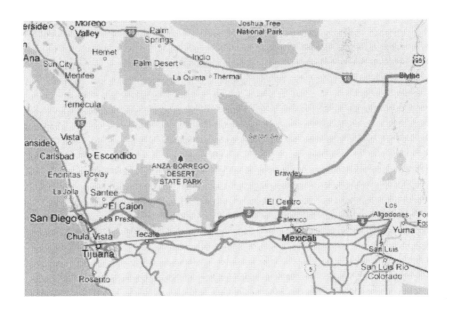

In-Ko-Pah Gorge

Zipping down In-Ko-Pah Gorge on Interstate 8 east of San Diego is a beautiful drive. After climbing over mountains getting away from the coast, you now have a graceful, curvy road to coast down at 70 miles per hour. In just a few miles you travel from being just under a mile high to sea level and below. Driving a Corvette with the top down would be an exhilarating experience. However, standing by my bike with the traffic whizzing by on the interstate just a couple of feet to my left, it looked like a harrowing and daunting ride.

Just ahead of where I stood with my bike, I noticed a large sign warning *CAUTION – HIGH CROSS WINDS.* The wind was blasting Helen and me as we hung on to our bikes to keep from being blown into the ditch. Looking ahead I could see places where the right shoulder of the road dropped off hundreds of feet to the bottom of the gorge. The landscape was a barren, brown desert almost totally devoid of vegetation. Huge, rounded boulders dotted the steep mountain side. The look was chaotic and surreal. Getting to the bottom of this gorge on our bikes was not going to be at all like our Florida training rides on A1A.

This could be dangerous. Using our brakes while trying to control a safe and sane speed could heat the rims of the wheels causing a tire to blow. Changing a tire on the shoulder of this

22

interstate highway was not something I desired to do. I didn't even want to think about the consequences of a fall.

It was only our second day on the road. After starting by riding west to San Diego the day before, we were now heading east, and I was faced with something that frightened me. What were my options? Helen was raring to go. She encouraged me as I tried to convince her it was very dangerous, and perhaps I'd just walk down

Before we left home, a friend and member of our church in Melbourne Beach, Doris Ballou, had suggested I adopt Joshua 1:9 as my theme Bible verse for this ride. *Have I not commanded you? Be strong and courageous. Do not be frightened, and do not be dismayed, for the Lord your God is with you wherever you go.* (ESV) At the top of In-Ko-Pah Gorge on Interstate-8, remembering that verse, and knowing that God was with me, even here, was a great comfort. Pulling out all the courage I could, I finally mounted the bike and started riding down the frightening gorge behind Helen.

I had read that bikes are permitted on some interstates when there are no other options for getting from point A to point B. There was only one way down the gorge and we were on it. The shoulder was wide and gave us what amounted to a bike lane all the way down. It didn't take long to get to the point where I was able to ignore the traffic, and concentrate on getting down this steep gorge in good health. My fear of our being blown into the traffic was not justified since the wind was blowing from our left and across the highway. The threat was being blown off the road on the right and to the bottom of the gorge. The traffic

23

gave us plenty of room. Some drivers even gave us a little toot and thumbs up as they went by demonstrating their respect for the difficulty of the task we had undertaken.

Helen holding on to the bikes during a tire cooling break

I followed Helen who seemed much surer of herself. It was a weird experience watching her make a sweeping turn to the right while leaning to the left into the wind. Helen would stop about every ten minutes, and we'd admire the stark desert landscape as we let our wheels cool off. We were doing no pedaling. A rest stop wasn't needed, but the hot wheels verified we'd been riding the brakes to keep the bikes under control. After a few minutes, they'd be cooled off, and we'd get back on the bikes easing our way down another half mile for our next break.

At last, we exited Interstate-8 at the bottom of the gorge. Before us appeared a desolate landscape. Down the road to our left we could see a few trees and scattered buildings. Our Adventure Cycling Southern Tier Route Map identified this as the Yuha Desert and the scattered buildings were the town of Ocotillo. The map also listed the Ocotillo Trailer Park and Motel as a place for lodging.

We rode our bikes the mile north and found the Ocotillo Trailer Park and Motel as we entered the town. This was not an inviting place to spend our first night on the road. My guess is it started as tourist cabins in the 1930's or 40's. As the cabins decayed and were torn down, the vacant lots became spots for RVs and mobile homes. We decided to ride further into town to see if perhaps our map had missed the new Holiday Inn.

The town was dusty and the houses all seemed to need a fresh coat of paint. The desert climate had not been kind to Ocotillo. It was almost like the town was trying to conceal itself in the dust and sand. The town seemed shy or embarrassed. The few scrubby trees were the only vegetation. There was a store near what might have been the center of the town. We stopped to see if we could get information about lodging options, and to pick up some food for our dinner. The people were friendly enough, and let us know the Ocotillo Trailer Park and Motel was our only choice.

Checking in at the motel, we secured a cabin for the night. The woman manager was very friendly and interested in our adventure. Her husband came up and got into the conversation. He looked like he had spent a lot of time in the desert. His face was deeply wrinkled and showed signs of frequent sunburn. He had several days' worth of whiskers and his hair hung down

25

over his collar. Learning this was our first time in the desert, he got into a story telling mode sharing some of his experiences. We talked about our route through the desert, and he suggested we stay off what would be the shorter route to our next stopping point, El Centro. Our proposed road had no shoulders. When he said we would run into a lot of truck traffic hauling drywall from a nearby factory, we were convinced. He gave good advice, and we followed it.

Our room that night was very basic to say the least. Our sleep was disturbed during the night by the noise from the wind that came howling down from the mountains we had crossed. Not only did the windows on the west rattle, they kept very little of the wind and accompanying dust out of the room. The curtains were blowing out almost perpendicular, and all we could do was lie in bed and listen. The temperature also plummeted, and we began emptying our packs to find extra clothes.

I assured Helen the wind would die down as soon as it got light. Was I ever wrong? If anything, it got stronger. We finally took the bikes outside, put on the panniers, and started to ride. After about two feet of riding, we both dismounted. The wind in our faces was just too strong. We walked the fifty yards out to the highway, and were finally able to start riding to the south with the wind blasting our right side. The route for the day would be turning east in a couple of miles. I assured Helen we would have a great rest of the day with this high wind pushing us east to the Imperial Valley. I lost more credibility when we turned east at the same time the wind died.

26

Traveling in a car, we would never have stopped in the town of Ocotillo, much less have stayed in a cabin at the trailer park/motel. On the bike, we didn't have the option to pass it up and look for a better place. This trip was already changing our lives by getting us out of our comfort zone!

As we lay in bed in Ocotillo listening to the wind and shivering, we talked about how difficult this ride was going to be, and questioned whether or not we would be able to make it. After the day riding down In-Ko-Pah Gorge and then the night in the desert cabin, we were wondering if we could really finish what we had just started. We needed to be strong and courageous, and take it a day at a time. Spending a night in a cabin in the desert was the first of many steps

Ready to leave our cabin in Ocotillo

The Border Patrol and Illegal Immigrants

Our safety as we rode along close to the Mexican border the first three days of our adventure had been a topic of conversation long before we departed. As I write this in 2012, Mexico is in a brutal and bloody war between the drug cartels and the government. Northern Mexico and the frontier is a dangerous place with daily reports of gun battles being fought in the cities and villages. There were plenty of people sneaking across the border from Mexico in 2001, and a lot of drugs were being smuggled into the U.S., but the threat of violence was much less then than it is now.

There were places on our first three days of riding where we were riding very close to the border. In fact, at one point the fence separating the two countries was on the shoulder of the road. However, we never felt in danger. Border Patrol officers were everywhere. The first two days, I don't think we were ever out of the view of at least one of them. You could see officers sitting on rocks on the hills looking out on the rugged landscape with binoculars. Their SUVs and pick-ups accounted for most of the traffic. At one of the Border Patrol check-points, where we stopped for a rest, I mentioned our route to an officer. He just smiled and said something about knowing exactly where we were riding. In fact, he mentioned they had been expecting us. It was reassuring to know someone was watching out for us.

I was curious to know what the people who live and work along the border thought of the people who were sneaking into the country rather than entering legally. In a little country general store near the village of Potrero, Helen and I had

28

stopped for a rest on our first day. I struck up a conversation with the proprietor, and asked about his thoughts on the issue. He said occasionally a person sneaking in would stop at the store. Pointing south out the front of the store, he said, "it is only a couple of miles over the mountain to Mexico, but you wouldn't believe how beat up these people are after having walked over that mountain and through the desert." I sensed he was very concerned about their welfare.

The attitude of the desert man I spoke with at the motel in Ocotillo was similar. One of his desert stories was about how he and his buddies like to take their desert buggies out driving off the roads in the desert. They seldom saw any people. However, occasionally an *Illegal* would stop at the motel and ask for water. Like the man in Potrero, he commented on the poor physical condition of those who stop. He said he always asked if they wanted him to call the Border Patrol to pick them up. The BP officers had told him they would take them to their compound where they would be given a good meal, and then delivered back to Mexico. Some asked him to call, but most didn't want to stop, saying they had a promise of work in Las Angeles. He asked if they knew how to get to Las Angeles? They would just point north, get a drink, and head back out into the desert.

This man also told how he and his friends put up flags on PVC pipes in the desert, and placed jugs of water by them for the *illegals* who were struggling through. They would go out every few days with tanks of water and refill jugs. He reported they never saw anyone, but the jugs were almost always empty.

29

He said, "These are just poor people trying to find work." To his way of thinking, they were all there because of their poor economic condition in Mexico. They were desperate to find a way to provide for their family. He would rather fill water jugs than find dead bodies.

At our first stop in Arizona, the motel operator told a story about a tragedy that had happened near there a day or two before we arrived. Some laborers in the local vegetable fields slept during the night in a dry creek bed. There had been rain up in the mountains miles to the north one day, but no rain fell anywhere near where the men were working. While they slept that night, walls of water swept down the dry creek bed. All were carried away and drowned. The county sheriff recovered the bodies the next day. The bodies had no identification papers, and no one knew how to contact their families. The story teller commented that the people in the area were concerned knowing there were families somewhere who had lost husbands and fathers, and there was no way to notify them or to even return the bodies.

These stories all illustrate how in 2001 the people I met on the Mexican border expressed more compassion for the welfare of those entering the country illegally than danger from the violence in Mexico. I have to wonder what those people would say about that now, ten years later as we get the daily reports of gun battles along the border.

On our third day on the road, we had spent the morning riding through the Yuha Desert after leaving Ocotillo. Riding down a little slope we left the barren desert and entered the lush

30

Imperial Valley. Helen and I stopped under the first tree we had seen all day to rest a bit in the shade. There was a dirt road entering the highway from the south next to where we had stopped. While we were resting in the cool shade, a Border Patrol vehicle came up the dirt road toward us. As the vehicle approached I noticed it was dragging tires behind. When the officer got to the highway where we were standing, he stopped, got out, and went back to load the tires in the back of his SUV. I walked over to ask what he was doing. He told me he was smoothing the road by dragging it with the tires. Later he will come back to see if any new foot prints were on the road. Any foot prints would have been made by someone sneaking into the country. He said the border was only about a mile to our south. I asked if there really were illegals in that area. We had been riding through the area for three days without seeing anyone. He assured us there were plenty of them around, but they were usually hiding during the day. About that time, he got a call on his radio that a man was walking along the road about a half mile ahead of us. His next job was to check on this man. He wished us well and drove off as we got back on our bikes. We had ridden about a quarter mile when he came driving back past us. In the back seat of the SUV was a man sitting behind the screened partition. This was confirmation of what he had told us.

The Yuha Desert

Being Cheered On

We had been on the road for three days and were still learning how to make this adventure work. A concern that was always in the back of our minds was where we could find lodging each night. At this early stage in the trip, we were looking ahead to what was available at various places on our route according to our Adventure Cycling maps. A month later we were much more confident in our being able to vary from the prescribed tour route, and not find ourselves in an impossible situation. However, at the time we were in the Imperial Valley of California, we hadn't gotten to that level of confidence.

Sitting in a motel in El Centro, we were planning how we would get out of California. We had maps for the route, but there is more to traveling than knowing what road to take. While a five mile ride in a car to get a drink of water would not be a big deal, on a bike, in the desert, those five miles could be serious trouble.

Looking ahead on our route, the town of Brawley was about 20 miles north of El Centro, and still in the Imperial Valley. After Brawley, we would have a ride east in the Imperial Valley for about 20 miles before we got back in desert and turned northeast. Another 50 plus miles would get us to the small town of Palo Verde and from there it was a little over 20 miles to Blythe. We would cross the Colorado River east of Blythe and enter Arizona.

The young people riding the Southern Tier Route would make El Centro to Blythe in one day. That would be more of a day than we cared to put in. Being old retirees we didn't feel it necessary to do a 100 mile day, and besides, there might be some interesting things along the way we'd want to explore.

Our decision that day was to make the ride to Brawley in one day, and ride on to Palo Verde the day after that. Short rides appealed to me.

Riding north out of El Centro, we discovered the Imperial County Historical Society Pioneer Museum. Since this was going to be a short riding day, we had time to stop, and check it out. Our entrance into the museum wearing our cycling attire created quite a stir. People don't usually wear neon yellow jerseys when they visit a museum. We were the only visitors

33

that morning and the staff was very eager to talk about our ride from San Diego and where we were going after El Centro. They made us feel very special and welcome. In fact, they treated us like celebrities.

When I saw they had a computer, I asked if they had internet access. One of my college friends, Herman Sieck, had been posting my daily emails on the Owls60 website. I hadn't seen his postings. I was sending my emails using a little mailstation that didn't have internet capability. (The Owls was our social group at Cornell College and Herm is our group website guru.) The staff at the museum was as excited to see the web postings as we were. It was an interesting experience to look on the internet, and actually see what I had been writing about our adventure. As we left, the museum staff assured us they would be following along on their computer as we rode home to Florida.

While we were of interest to the museum staff, we found the museum to be interesting to us. Learning how this valley below sea level has become such a lush agricultural area was worth the stop. We never would have had that experience if we had been in a hurry to get to Palo Verde or Blythe.

Riding north from the museum, we passed through the town of Imperial. There are tall grain elevators on the right as you enter the town from the south. Growing up in Iowa, I've seen many large grain elevators, but what got my attention in Imperial was what was written on them. About 50 feet up was a horizontal line with the words "sea level." At that time, I was as low as I've ever been.

34

Just past the elevators, I saw what looked like an elementary school on our right. There was a fence separating the school playground from the four-lane highway we were pedaling north on. I pointed out the school to Helen, and commented that it looked like lunch recess.

Both of us worked in elementary schools and lunch recess was something with which I was very familiar. In fact, my varicose veins were earned standing watch for years over children playing during their lunch recess.

As we were passing the school, we heard cheering. When we looked to see where the cheering was coming from, we saw the children running to the fence cheering loudly and shouting, "God Bless you." WOW!! What a boost that was! We waved to the kids, and I sat a little taller as we rode on down the road with tears rolling down my cheeks; their cheers pushing us along.

Our fourth day on the road, and being treated special by both the staff in the museum and the kids at the school, reinforced our feeling this adventure was going to be a life changing experience.

Larry and Rudy on the Road to Palo Verde

As Helen and I rode east out of Brawley starting our fifth day on the road, in my rearview mirror I noticed two riders overtaking us. As they came along side, we began to chat about where we were all going, and where we had been. They

35

introduced themselves as Larry Terbush and Rudy Saul from Santa Rosa, California.

In the Imperial Valley

Larry and Rudy were also following the Southern Tier Route, and had begun today's ride in El Centro. Their goal for the day was Palo Verde, the same as ours.

Larry and Rudy were on vacation, and had a limited number of days to ride. Their plan was to ride as far as possible this spring, and finish the ride from that point in September. They were the first bike tourists we had seen, although we had heard others were not far ahead. At our rate, we'd never overtake anyone.

It was enjoyable to ride along with Larry and Rudy exchanging stories and sharing experiences we'd had in preparation for the adventure. After riding together for several

36

miles, they were eager to speed up, so we all said goodbye. They were soon out of sight.

A few miles later, we overtook them at the south entrance to the Imperial Dunes Recreation Area. On some maps we have seen this called the Algodones Dunes Wilderness Area and the locals refer to it as the Glamis Dunes. Whatever you call it, it's something unusual. I was told when a movie company is looking for a location that looks like the Sahara Desert, this is where they come. The dunes are massive piles of sand. They stretch from north of where we entered them on highway 78 all the way south to near Yuma, Arizona, and the Mexican border.

With the exception of the irrigated Imperial Valley, we had been riding through desert since In-Ko-Pah Gorge, but that desert didn't look like the Imperial Dunes. There was absolutely no vegetation, just sand. It went on for almost 10 miles. The other deserts had scrub bushes and cactus, some of which were blooming with pretty, delicate flowers. These dunes didn't have anything green.

We stopped to talk with Larry and Rudy, and Helen took our picture. They were ready to leave as we stopped, so after a short visit we all again said goodbye, and they headed for Palo Verde as we peddled our way through the dunes slowly following them. Near the end of the dunes and just outside the Recreation Area, we came to what I thought was going to be a town; Glamis. I was surprised the *town* just turned out to be a store surrounded by old trailers and RVs scattered around the sand. The name on the front of the building was *Glamis Beach Store.* When we pointed out to the people in the store we lived at a beach and Glamis wasn't exactly what we thought of as a beach, they just laughed and said they only lacked one thing, water. The people there enjoy playing in the sand, and I think they even ride surf boards down the dunes. They can call it a beach if they want.

As we rode out of the dunes we entered a section of highway with signs that warned of "dips." This area was like riding over the Melbourne Causeway upside down. I tried to get up enough speed going down a dip to carry me to the top of the next one and then I'd fly down that one. The first half of this section we actually gained over a thousand feet in elevation. We then lost most of the elevation before our ride for the day ended in Palo Verde. I'm sure the warning signs for the dips were in case of rain when they might fill with water. I can't believe they get much rain in this desert, but when they do it might be a real *gulley washer* or in this case a *dip washer*

After another 20 or 30 miles we again saw Larry and Rudy as we arrived at a Border Patrol check point just as they were leaving. Again we greeted, and then said goodbye as they headed on to Palo Verde while we stopped for some water and conversation with the lonely Border Patrol agents. There was very little traffic on this road for them to check, so we got royal treatment once more

Helen is riding through the dunes.

We finally arrived in Palo Verde about 2 p.m. Guess what! Larry and Rudy were just walking out of Big Jack's Café/Bar. After eating and resting for a while, they felt like riding some more, and had decided to go on to Blythe for the night. We told them we were going to spend the night here in Palo Verde at the campground. For the fourth time that day we told them goodbye, and wished them well, knowing that would be the last we'd see each other.

While Palo Verde was the last we saw of them, it wasn't our last contact. Two days later, we were in Quartzite, Arizona. I asked the manager of the one motel in town if Larry and Rudy had stopped there the night before. She said they had stopped to eat in the restaurant, but hadn't stayed. They told her they were going to ride on to Salome to spend the night.

The next day, as we headed to Salome from Quartzite, Helen and I stopped at the Kofa Café for lunch. This café is at a crossroads out in the middle of nowhere. It was somewhat busy when we stopped, and I got the idea that the restaurant had a lot of business since it was the only place you could eat within many miles. While there, I went to the restroom. To keep people from marking up the wall with graffiti and notes, the restaurant had put a white board on the restroom wall along with a marker. People left notes and comments on this board. As I was doing what I'd gone to the room for, I read the comments, and was shocked to see in rather large print, "Hi Frank, from Larry and Rudy." When I returned to our table Helen was very curious why I was laughing coming out of the restroom

While we didn't actually see Larry and Rudy again, we did get some progress reports, and know they got well into Texas in April. In September, they returned and finished their cross-continent ride.

The Madam's Room and an Emmy Award

We carried a small tent and light weight sleeping bags, knowing from our Southern Tier Route maps there would be nights where we would not find a motel. We got to one of those places after the long ride from Brawley to Palo Verde. In fact, this turned out to be one of the longest rides on our entire adventure; over 70 miles. Our maps only listed campgrounds in Palo Verde. There was also a bold faced note on the map: *"SERVICES ARE EXTREMELY LIMITED BETWEEN BRAWLEY AND PALO VERDE. PLAN ACCORDINGLY AND*

CARRY FOOD AND WATER. BE PREPARED TO CAMP BY THE ROAD IF NECESSARY." There was only one other place on our entire route where we had a warning like this, and that was a great story I'm looking forward to sharing with you in the next chapter.

We rolled into the town just as Larry and Rudy were getting on their bikes outside Big Jack's Café/Bar. They said the food was okay, so we went in for lunch while they rode out of town heading for Blythe. It seemed like a good idea to get some food before heading out to the campground by the Colorado River.

As we were getting back on our bikes after eating at Big Jack's, Helen noticed a sign about a hundred yards ahead of us: *Lagoon Lodge.* The word *Lodge* got our attention. It sounds like a place where you might find a room for the night. I went back into the restaurant and asked Big Jack if the Lagoon Lodge had motel rooms. He said he thought they had a couple rooms. We decided to investigate.

There didn't seem to be an office or any sign indicating where to check-in at the Lagoon Lodge. The Lagoon Saloon seemed to be associated with the Lodge, so Helen stayed with the bikes while I went in the saloon to see if they could help us. The bartender said they had four rooms. One was available that night. When I asked where they were, he pointed out the window to a building that looked like an antique store and said, "I'll give you the Madam's room." I'm sure he said that to get a rise out of me, and I didn't disappoint him. He chuckled as he knew I was wondering just what kind of place I was getting into.

Not many motels where we would want to stay have a Madam's room.

Palo Verde, California

He then explained, "You have probably heard of the Hollywood Madam scandal. Well, the Madam in that scandal hid from the police for a month in that room. While here, she was running her operation using the room phone. After she was arrested, I got this huge phone bill. She wouldn't pay and neither would I, so the phone company took the phone out of the room. You won't have a phone tonight."

I assured him we could get by for a night without a phone, especially if it meant not having to set up our camping gear.

This actually turned out to be a nice, large room. It was more like an apartment than a motel room. There was a full eat-in kitchen, a living room, bedroom, and bath. I thought it would be a good place to hide from the law for a month.

That evening, we went back to Big Jack's Café/Bar for dinner. While we had been the only ones there in the afternoon, it was now packed. We went to the back where we took the last empty table.

It was obvious we were strangers. The regular customers were trying to ignore us, but it became obvious we were a curiosity. Palo Verde is not a tourist Mecca by any means. With what happened with the Madam, the regulars may have suspected we were some sort of secret agents. Finally, someone came over and asked who we were?

The Madam's Room

When we told them we were from Florida, and had left San Diego a few days before on bikes heading for home, we were mobbed. Everyone gathered around, and started peppering us with questions. Obviously, we weren't like the young people they were used to seeing riding through their town on the bike route we were following. We were more like the Palo Verdeans.

43

People they could identify with. They all seemed to be thinking that if gray haired retirees could do this, maybe I'm not too old for some adventure.

The ladies flocked around Helen like she was a movie star. They kept asking her questions until I finally pulled her away explaining to her fans she needed her rest. I reminded them we had more miles to cover the next day. They let us go (after I paid our bill) with many good wishes for a successful adventure. We might have been the biggest thing to hit Palo Verde since the Madam was arrested.

The next day we rode through farm land rather than desert. From Palo Verde to Blythe, we were in the Colorado River Valley. Irrigation here had made the desert bloom much like the Imperial Valley. It was a relatively short day of riding, but we told ourselves we needed a little rest after the hard riding through the dunes the previous day. This would be our last day in California, and we still hadn't met a movie star. Blythe didn't seem like a place to find stars. We didn't have high expectations.

About 20 miles north of Palo Verde, our route crossed over Interstate Highway 10. We then turned east on what was probably the old highway. Before the interstate, this was a heavily traveled road. Now all the traffic and business has moved to the interstate. When we got into Blythe, we were on the main business street in the pre-interstate days. Like many towns near a major interstate highway, many of the businesses and motels have moved to the interchanges, and the old downtown is struggling to stay alive. We peddled all the way

44

down this street eyeing the old motels. Some looked pretty run down, and a few were trying to keep up the appearance of modern motels. They were all having difficulty competing with the large chains like the Holiday Inns at the interchange. We got almost to the east side of the town when we were attracted to the Astro Motel. It looked clean, and there was something pleasing about its appearance that drew us in.

While Helen filled out the check-in form, I looked around the Astro lobby. On the wall were a number of framed autographed photos of Mary Tyler Moore and the other actors who were in her popular TV show many years ago. As I studied one photo in particular, there was a man being presented an Emmy Award who looked like the man behind the counter. When I asked about it, he confirmed he was indeed the man in the photo. He had won the Emmy as a writer for the Mary Tyler Moore Show.

His name was Ray Villareal. When the show went off the air, he had been offered jobs with other shows. However, he found the kind of writing the new shows wanted was not the kind of writing he was willing to do. The sex and foul language was just something he could not be a part of. He also was concerned about raising his children in the Los Angeles area, so he moved to Blythe, and bought the Astro Motel.

We were ready to leave California, and while we didn't get to meet a movie star, we did meet a very moral man who stood by his principles even after receiving one of the highest honors of show business. The next day we would reach a milestone as we crossed our first state line.

Crossing the Colorado River

CHAPTER 3

ARIZONA
April 6 to April 18, 2001

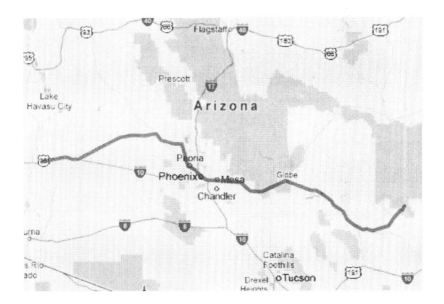

STOPPING IN SALOME

Crossing the state line into Arizona was both a physical and emotional milestone. As we rode the bikes over the pedestrian lane attached to the Interstate 10 Bridge crossing the Colorado River, we realized this adventure was getting serious. The safety net that we might have thought we had in California with our son and my sister living there, was now gone. We only knew one person in the whole state of Arizona, and she was miles ahead of us.

After crossing the bridge, we had to enter Interstate 10. This was the only road east. It was a good ride with plenty of room on the shoulder for our bikes. Riding on interstate highways can be very noisy. The big SUVs with the knobby tires make a lot of racket. When they are approaching from the rear, you hear them long before you see them. They sure aren't a surprise when they roar past.

The route all day seemed to be uphill as we left the Colorado River Valley for another short day of riding to the town of Quartzite. This was almost a ghost town the day we stopped. A month or two earlier there would have been thousands of people in and around town; most of them in RVs parked in the desert.

This is the place to be in the winter if you like to search for rocks and gems. It has become so popular; it is also now a huge winter flea market.

All the country we rode through in Arizona for the first several days was desert. This was not the sand dune desert, but was more of the scrub and cactus kind. One big difference between this desert and those in California was the saguaro cactus. This is the very tall cactus with lots of arms. We had seen nothing like this in California.

As we pedaled along we were almost always riding in single file. When I was in the lead, Helen liked to get up real close and "draft" by taking advantage of my shielding her from the head wind. I didn't like drafting. The person in the lead has a responsibility to let the drafter know when a pot hole or road kill is in the way. When I followed, I preferred to stay 10 to 20 yards back.

This way I could look around at the scenery without fear of running over Helen. In drafting, the person behind had to be very careful not to get so close her front wheel overlapped the rear of the leader. We learned later in the trip why overlapping is very bad.

With all this concentration and distance between us, conversation while we were riding was at a minimum. Our frequent stops gave us plenty of chance to talk about what we had seen and were experiencing.

A giant saguaro cactus

. These stops came every time we got to a place with a restroom and/or cold drinks and snacks.

The maps that covered the western states had a "route elevation profile" showing the ups and downs of our route. At every stop in California and Arizona, Helen took the map out of my handlebar bag. She checked to see how much we had been climbing, and what was ahead. This was interesting information, but it wasn't very useful. If the road went up, we didn't have any options but to pedal harder and in a lower gear.

The ride from Quartzite to Salome (the natives pronounce it Sa-loam) took us through several small towns. At one convenience store stop, some people were standing around their cars talking. They reacted much like the people in Big Jack's Café/Bar in Palo Verde. One woman who was by a car with a Michigan license plate got very excited. She could hardly contain herself. Her reaction was like we were the movie stars we had missed seeing in California. As she jumped up and down with excitement she said, "I've heard of people doing things like that, but never thought I'd actually meet someone like you." I guess we made her day and gave her something to tell the folks back in Michigan.

When we rode into Salome after riding about 60 miles, we were ready to call it a day. Scouting out the town didn't take long. There was a school, and this gave the town something of a look of permanence. The couple of stores, a few houses, and RVs scattered around the area served to define it as a town.

Helen checking the elevation profile on our map.

There were two motels in Salome. A man in one of the convenience store stops that day recommended Shefflers Motel over the Westward Motel. Based on this recommendation by someone we didn't know, we stopped at Shefflers to get our room for the night. After checking-in, we went to see the room before touring the town to find where we could eat dinner. Walking in the room, Helen gave a gasp. Her first comment was, "taking a breath makes me feel like I just smoked a pack of cigarettes." Her next reaction was, "I'm not getting under those bed covers." I couldn't imagine what the Westward Motel would have been like if Shefflers was the best in town. We had already paid for the room based on the unknown person's recommendation, so we realized this was going to be home for that night whether we liked it or not.

Helen took everything out of her panniers and covered the bed, so none of her body would actually touch it. We then went to the only restaurant in town, and ordered a pizza from the limited menu. The restaurant was also a small grocery store. The manager took our order, walked over to the store's frozen food cooler, removed a frozen pizza, and popped it into the micro-wave oven. When the timer went off, we had our dinner!

What a night we had in Salome! To this day, when we find ourselves in a difficult or uncomfortable situation Helen will give me a knowing look and say, "Remember, we've been to Salome and survived." This was another big step in getting us out of our comfort zone, and set the bottom of the bar we still use to gauge motels.

Our First Arizona Angels

After stops in Quartzite, Salome, and Wickenburg, we arrived in the Phoenix area. This was by far the largest metropolitan area we pedaled through on this cross-continent adventure.

My mother and step-father (Dawson Cornish) had moved to Sun City on the west side of Phoenix shortly after their wedding. Sun City was developed by Del Webb in 1960 and was the first community that was restricted to residents at least 55 years old. Mom and Dawson loved Sun City, and had many friends there. Some of these friends Mom had known in Iowa. One of them, Beth Evans, had been our neighbor when I was growing up in Early, Iowa. Her husband, Bob, had also grown up in Early, and was a life-long friend of Mom's. In fact, Bob had been Best Man when Mom and Dad were married.

Remembering that Beth, now widowed, still lived part-time in Sun City, I had contacted her to let her know we were planning to pass through the Phoenix area. She insisted that we stop and stay a night with her. We were happy to accept her invitation.

Staying with Beth was the first time we had been in a home since starting our adventure. It was nice not to be staying in a motel. We were still trying to recover from Salome.

When Beth took us out for dinner, it was our first ride in a vehicle other than our bikes since Brad had dropped us off back at Tecate Divide in California. The dinner was a special treat because Beth had arranged for her sister-in-law, Shirley Ward, who I had forgotten lived in Sun City West, to join us.

Sitting with old friends from Early, Iowa, and talking about old times was fun. We were happy we'd stopped to see these gracious ladies from my old home town. In fact, we enjoyed it so much; we stayed for an extra day. This was our first of what turned out to be many *rest* days.

Beth drove us around during the rest day, and we located the spot where we would rejoin the Southern Tier Route map in the city of Glendale. We had relied heavily on the map to guide us through downtown San Diego as we were beginning this adventure, now we would rely on it to get us through this large metropolitan area.

Early in the morning on the day after our *rest*, we were on our bikes. Saying goodbye and thanks for the wonderful hospitality, we rode out of Sun City at dawn and pedaled over to the spot where we got back on our designated route.

Once on the route, we were surprised how well it had been planned. Riding a bike all the way through a large, unfamiliar city can be a daunting task. The route we rode took us almost 15 miles on a bike trail along the Arizona Canal to what I think was about the center of Phoenix. From the point we got off the bike trail, we rode on streets with a designated bike lane all the way to Tempe and the Arizona State University campus.

I was carrying a lot of extra inner tubes in case we had flat tires. The day we rode from Quartzite to Salome, I had noticed my rear tire was low, and I had to add air. It was the first time I'd needed to use the tire pump attached to my bike.

The next day I had to add air a couple more times, and the day after that I changed the tube thinking that would solve my problem. However, as we got on our bikes at Beth's, I again noticed my rear tire was low, and I added air to the new tube. A little later, the tire wasn't just low, it was flat! I again changed the tube and pedaled into Phoenix alongside the canal.

A few miles later, the bike trail ended, and we entered the city streets. At the first convenience store we passed, we stopped. While Helen was inside using the restroom, I sat on the curb watching the bikes. I hadn't been sitting there long when another bike rider, Taylor, pulled up on a shiny bike with a coffee cup in his hand. Taylor commented how easy it was to spot me with my bright neon yellow jersey. He asked the usual questions about what we were doing, and where we were going. As he was ready to go in for his morning coffee, he asked me how the bikes were working out. I told him they were great. I also mentioned I'd been having problems with flat tires. He had just told me he was working at a bike shop. When I mentioned the flats, he said, "Do you want to me to fix this problem?"

My first thought was, "You've got to be kidding me. Here I am, depending on that bike to get me home, and I'm going to let a perfect stranger in a 7-11 parking lot work on it." However, he seemed like a nice guy, and I felt I needed help, so I said, "Have at it."

I had to remove all of the panniers before Taylor could get to the rear tire. This meant when Helen walked out of the store, she saw me standing by a pile of panniers while a stranger was removing my rear wheel. Her mouth dropped open as she looked at me with an expression that I interpreted to mean something like, "Have you lost your mind letting this guy take your bike apart?"

Before Helen could get the words out, I said, "Honey, I want you to meet Taylor. He is a bike mechanic and volunteered to fix my rear tire so I don't keep getting the flats."

Later Helen told me, "As soon as I looked at the way Taylor was handling the bike, it was obvious he knew what he was doing."

When Taylor had the rear tire off the wheel, he very carefully examined the inner wall of the tire. I told him I'd already done that, and hadn't found a thing. He, however, did find the *thing* I'd missed. Somewhere along the way, probably while riding on Interstate 10 west of Quartzite, I had picked up a little piece of steel wire from a steel belted tire that had blown

56

out on a truck. If you've driven on any interstate highway you have seen the chunks of tires along the shoulder. A little piece of steel wire that had been on the shoulder of the road had worked its way into my tire. As I rode with that wire poking into the tube, it eventually created a small hole and the air escaped.

Taylor pulled out the wire, and then put the tire back on the wheel. This made the bike as good as new, almost. Taylor wasn't done. He asked if we had a 5mm Allen wrench. When I gave him one, he proceeded to give each of our bikes a little tune up.

When I asked Taylor what I could pay him, he told us he just likes working on bikes. "If you want to repay me," he said, "you can help someone out who you meet who is having trouble on the road."

I did go in the 7-11 and got a cup of coffee for Taylor. Then he, Helen, and I sat on the curb talking bikes. Taylor told us his story about being a racer, and trying to get on a Tour de France team. He was about there, and then had an accident that kept him off the bike for a while. He was working in the Phoenix bike shop to support himself as he tried to get back in racing condition.

We finally had to say goodbye to Taylor, so he could go to work, and so we could finish our ride through Phoenix on our way to Mesa for the night.

As Helen and I rode along and talked about Taylor, we realized that in the whole city of Phoenix he was the only person we met. If he hadn't stopped at the 7-11 at the same time we did, I'd still be fixing flats. We were certain the Lord had sent him to assure us He was looking out for us. As far as we were concerned, Taylor was a genuine angel.

Easter in Globe

After a night at a motel in Mesa, we headed east. About mid-morning, we finally left the metropolitan area of Phoenix. It seemed much more natural for us to be riding in the wide-open spaces rather than contending with the city traffic. I settled into a comfortable pedaling cadence. Suddenly I heard a "POP!" followed by "thump-thump-thump-thump." The sound was coming from right below me. Looking down I saw that the tire Taylor had so kindly worked on the day before had blown-out, and was now in pieces.

It didn't take long to figure out what happened. The tires have a bead running around their inner circumference that hooks under a ridge on the rim, and holds the tire in place. I had taken this tire off so many times in the past couple of days I had damaged this bead. With the pressure of the tube now holding air along with my weight, the tube forced the tire to separate from the bead. A little of the inner tube then slipped out of the tire, and was pinched between the tire and the rim. It hadn't taken long after I got up to speed for the tube to finally blow; tearing a big hole in the side of the tire.

In preparing for this adventure, I had stocked up not only on inner tubes, but I also had extra tires stashed deep in the panniers. These were knobby tires, not the smooth road tires I had been using, but in the desert east of Phoenix, a knobby tire was a whole lot better than a flat tire.

It didn't take me long to replace the blown tire, and we were soon back on the road. The old tire found its final resting place in a trash can when we stopped to rest at Florence Junction.

We had been gradually climbing ever since Phoenix and the Valley of the Sun. East from Florence Junction, it was no longer a gradual climb. We were getting into rugged mountains and mining country. After making it over one pass and knowing the road from there was steep, we decided to make our home for the night in Superior, the first real town we had come to in these mountains.

Like all the mountain towns in this area of Arizona, Superior was an old mining town. There was a very tall smoke stack dominating the sky line. The story we heard was this smoke stack was all that remained of an ore processing facility. Evidently the mines in Superior had closed down.

After we checked into the El Portal Motel, which was one star better than Salome, we rode on through the town to see what we would be contending with in the morning. About a quarter mile past the El Portal, there was a tunnel. As we examined it from the west end we made several observations. The first thing we noticed was that it was just two lanes wide with no shoulder. We will be riding in the traffic. The second thing was that from where we stood, we couldn't see light at the end of the tunnel. The third observation was that we would be entering the tunnel at the lower end, and it would be a climb to the other end; wherever it was.

Riding through a mountain tunnel was not something you experience in Florida. We had to figure out a strategy for attacking this new challenge. What we came up with was to leave at first light, so as to get through while there was little traffic. We wanted to be very visible for any cars in the tunnel, so in addition to our neon yellow jerseys we would use the lights we had brought with us. This would be the first time we'd used the lights. The final part of our strategy was to ride as fast as we could to keep our time in the tunnel to a minimum.

Early the next morning we were on the road implementing our strategy. We actually raced through the tunnel and pulled over to the shoulder at the upper end with a great feeling of accomplishment, congratulating each other on our sprinting while going uphill carrying a full load. Little did we know the tunnel was not the toughest part of that day's ride.

As I'm writing this, I'm looking at the "Route Elevation Profile" on the map for this section of our route. It is nearly a vertical line. After the tunnel this was an extremely steep section of road. On top of it being steep, the road was narrow with no shoulder. We were pedaling in our lowest gear weaving across the road to make headway. It turned into a hike and bike day.

There were places it was so steep we had to walk and push the bike uphill. When the road became a little less vertical, we would get back on, and pedal until we literally hit the wall.

This is the end of the tunnel where we exited.

Traffic was light, but every time a car came up behind us, we had to stop weaving. This often forced us to a stop pedaling. The wind was also blowing down the mountain in our faces. After three and a half hours, we had gone just 10 miles.

We were "toast" and it wasn't even noon. We were also now looking at a steep descent like In-Ka-Pah Gorge. We took a rest at the top, and discussed where we wanted to make our home that night. This was Good Friday, so we also looked at the map for a likely place to spend Easter.

We were about 15 miles from the town of Globe. The next town of any size was Stafford, and it was almost a hundred miles ahead of us. We decided to stop over in Globe for a rest day, and then an additional day to be able to go to church on Easter. Stafford became our destination for the day after Easter.

With Globe as our goal, we did a lot of coasting through mining country. There were huge piles of green and white tailings left over from copper ore that had been taken out of the open-pit mines we were gliding past. When I mentioned the virtual mountains of tailings to a local in Globe, I was told with new processes, companies have gone back to these tailings, and are now extracting gold, silver and copper from what had been considered waste material a few years ago.

Once we got settled in the Globe Comfort Inn, I decided it was time to clean the grit and dirt off our bikes. I called a bike shop and talked with David who told me he had closed the shop a couple of months before. However, he had the items I needed to clean the bike. In a few minutes, he knocked on our door to deliver them. The charge was $10, but when I looked at the cleaning kit, the price was $13.99. I offered to pay the $13.99, but David wouldn't take it saying he was giving us a deal because he knew what we had just been through.

For our rest day, we didn't get on our clean bikes. To get around Globe, we called The Globe Taxi, and were picked up by Fred who was our driver for the day. Fred left us off at some old ruins. He then came back and took us to the local Safeway. There was a possibility we'd be camping once we got back on the road, so we got some camping food just in case.

Here is part of what our map had to say about the ruins we visited:

The ruins of the Besh-Ba-Gowah pueblo are located near Globe, Arizona, once a bawdy, rip-snorting copper mining town, and now a more sedate trade center.

62

The pueblo, covering two acres on a bluff overlooking Pinal Creek, was abandoned by its former occupants nearly 600 years ago, more than two centuries before Columbus discovered America. The name was given to the area by the Apache tribe, which arrived on the scene some 200 years after the pueblo was deserted. Roughly translated, Besh-Ba-Gowah means "place of metal."

Going through the pueblo was an interesting change of pace. Stopping in Globe was turning out to be a good decision.

Besh-Ba-Gowah

Looking in the phone book for a church to celebrate Easter with fellow Christians, we saw that Maranatha Baptist Church was just a ways down the highway from the Comfort Inn. We called to find out the time for their Easter service. Pastor Blake

63

Lasslett gave us the time, and said he'd be looking for us in the morning.

Resurrection Sunday dawned beautifully as we got back on our bikes after the rest day, and pedaled down the road to Maranatha Baptist Church. The Pastor was indeed looking for us, and had evidently clued in some of the members. They made us feel very welcome.

It was a very nice Easter service, but when it concluded we were informed that it wasn't over. The whole congregation was going out to a ranch for Easter lunch, and we were expected to join them. In fact, Larry and Mary Toner had already signed up for the job of following us back to the Comfort Inn where we were to leave our bikes, and then ride with them out to Vern and Josie Doreksen's ranch.

While the pot-luck lunch was good, the wonderful fellowship made the day special. We hated to finally have to say goodbye to these friendly people. They had made our Easter a special memory. In my email journal that day, Helen included a special note: "My special thanks to the wonderful 'sisters' I got to know who said they would be praying for us. How terrific it is to know we have more 'family' in Arizona."

The Doreksen's had the perfect facility for the picnic. This was a genuine Western barbeque.

Maranatha Baptist Church, Globe, Arizona

65

An Angel named Carla

It was Monday, the day after Easter, as we rode out of Globe with wonderful memories of our Easter with Maranatha Baptist Church. Our last look at Globe came as we passed the church, and started the glide down into the Gila River Valley.

While in Globe we happened to watch a movie on the TV in our Comfort Inn room about the Apache warrior, Geronimo. Most of this day was spent riding through the San Carlos Apache Reservation, and even through a little town named Geronimo. We were seeing the country we had just watched in the movie.

The ups and downs on the road today were more gradual than the last day we had ridden. The road was fairly flat for long stretches. While we pedaled over 80 miles, it was not as rigorous as the much shorter ride out of Superior. However, it seemed that the Arizona State Highway Department didn't want it to be too easy a ride. They *booby trapped* the highway by taking the nice wide shoulder, and making all but the outside two feet into a rumble strip. This meant riding on the shoulder required staying on a narrow strip of smooth asphalt. On our left was the deep rumble strip that could easily cause the front wheel to suddenly turn, throwing the rider off the bike. On the right, the desert sand eagerly awaited to grab the front wheel.

We were doing well, keeping out of the rumble strips and the sand, when we got to a short stretch with a steel guardrail on the right. It was attached to posts placed in the ground right at the edge of the paved shoulder. The guardrail itself was hanging about six inches over the shoulder. Our riding surface now was not much more than a foot wide. With our panniers hanging on the side, we were being squeezed.

I was riding a few yards ahead of Helen when I heard a loud "WHANG!" Looking back at Helen in my rearview mirror, I saw her lying on the shoulder of the road up against the guardrail. Obviously, the sound I heard was made by a plastic bike helmet slamming into a steel guardrail.

Helen was sitting up checking her moving parts to make sure they worked properly when I finally got back to her. She had gotten thrown off her bike by a rumble strip as she tried to keep her distance from the guardrail. We thanked the Lord she was unhurt except for a little scrape on her knee. We also determined to ride on the road rather than the *booby trapped* shoulder.

Riding along through the Gila River Valley was a pleasant ride except for the incident I just described. Besides riding through Geronimo, we also went through the town of Pima where the people were very proud to let us know they were the home of the very best cotton in the whole world.

Home that night was Stafford. As soon as we arrived we began to make preparations for the next couple of legs of this adventure. Now we were at the next place on our map after Palo Verde with a warning. This one in bold type said, *"Services are limited between Stafford, Arizona and Silver City, New Mexico. Carry extra food and water. Be prepared to camp by the road if necessary."* Between the local bike shop where I replenished our supply of inner tubes and Wal-Mart where we bought food, we left Stafford prepared to camp by the road if necessary.

In my email journal, I described the next day as "a tough day mentally." After leaving Stafford, we picked up highway 191, and rode on it the rest of that day. With the wind in our faces, we were climbing even though at times it looked like we should be going downhill. I stopped pedaling a couple of times thinking I would coast, and I just stopped. It must have been an optical illusion that made me think I was pedaling downhill.

This road finally descended to a long bridge over the Gila River. A mountain climb we had been warned about, stared us in the face. It was nearly as steep as what we had to climb leaving Superior, but it was longer and higher. The highest we got between Superior and Globe was about 4500 feet. The pass we were now scanning was 6300 feet. We decided to wait until the next morning to take on this challenge.

There was a little store and gas station at the east side of the bridge. Our map had the symbol for a campground at this intersection, but we couldn't see it. After inquiring in the store, we rode south along the Gila River until we found the Ponderosa RV Park. For a night, we could call our bikes RVs, so we pulled in, and claimed a camp site. The Ponderosa was almost deserted that night. .

As we were setting up our tent for the first time on this adventure, Helen expressed her feelings of concern about our ability to make it over the pass that was looming above us. The difficulty with the Superior to Globe ride was still fresh on her mind. I tried to encourage her with the facts that if we were ever going to get to our home in Florida; we had to make it over these mountains that kept getting in our way. They were no

68

surprise. These were what we had been reading about as we prepared for this adventure. We just had to take them on, be tough, and do the best we could. That might have been the thing to say as a football coach, but camping beside the Gila River with my wife, I wasn't very persuasive.

After listening to me and rejecting my logical argument, Helen came up with a plan. She was sure we could find someone nearby who would be going over the mountain in the morning. This person could take our panniers for us, and leave them off somewhere on the other side of the mountain. I'm sure I didn't tell her this was a ridiculous idea, but I did try to point out that in a place where we had not seen a living human since we rode south off the highway, the likelihood of finding the pannier transporter was *pie in the sky*.

The subject was dropped as we proceeded to get our camp/home set up for the night. We have been campers since we were first married and always enjoyed tenting. While we hadn't wanted to have to do this, we didn't mind camping for a night.

After about an hour in the camp, Susan Austin, who runs the campground, came to collect the camping fee. She sat and visited with us for a while. We learned that while we didn't need to worry about bears while we were camping, she did say skunks could be a problem. That gave me something else to worry about.

I mentioned to Susan I had seen some goats up on the cliff behind her home. She said they were the family *pack goats*. She and her husband like to hike, and the goats like to go along.

Her husband has taken advantage of the goats' interest in hiking by making little backpacks for each goat. Now when they hike, the goats carry all the food, water, and camping gear.

Helen then popped the question. Did Susan know of anyone who could carry her panniers over the mountain in the morning? Susan's response surprised me. Instead of laughing at this ridiculous idea, as I expected, she said it was possible. She'd ask around.

As I surveyed the campground, I didn't see any one for Susan to ask, but her response brought a smile to Helen's face. She hoped now that perhaps her plan could work even though I'd pooh-poohed it.

Helen preparing her nest at the Ponderosa

A few minutes later, Susan returned announcing that Carla Reeves will be driving over the mountain in the morning, and would be happy to take our panniers. She explained that Carla's husband works in a nearby copper mine. During the week he lives in his camper at the Ponderosa. Carla had come over that day to deliver a tool her husband needed, and was spending the night. She suggested we go down to talk with the Reeves.

I don't recall Helen looking at me and saying, "I told you so." She had been right, and I was happy to have been wrong.

Helen couldn't get to the Reeves' camper fast enough. They answered our knock, and Carla and Wayne came out to talk with us at their picnic table. Of course, the big issue was where was Carla going to take our panniers, and where would we find them.

According to my map, coming down off the pass towering above us, the road enters New Mexico. About 12 miles into New Mexico, is the town of Mule Creek. Another 20 miles past Mule Creek, is the town of Buckhorn. We asked Carla for her advice as the best place for us to regain the panniers. She said Mule Creek wasn't much of a town, but she knew Dave and Betty Morgan who ran the general store in Buckhorn. They have a few camp sites out behind the store. Her idea was to stop to see the Morgans, and drop off the panniers at the store. She suggested we call the Morgans, so they would be expecting her and us. We had some cell phone service, so we called. After talking with the Morgans, we felt everyone was on the up and up, and our bags would be delivered as planned.

That night I had trouble getting to sleep in our little tent. I had to protect Helen and our bikes from skunks. The next day I was going to trust a perfect stranger with all the gear we were counting on to get us home to Florida. On top of that, we had a mountain pass looming over us with a near vertical line on our map's profile chart for our day's ride. There was plenty to worry about and to keep me awake. I also thought about the 661 miles we'd covered in the nineteen days since San Diego. During that time we'd gained a lot of confidence in being able to get out of our comfort zone, and take on challenges. Now we were about to leave Arizona and our angels, and go into New Mexico. In my studying of our route maps, I was sure we would not be staying on the Southern Tier Route through New Mexico. Where we would leave the route was an unknown that night. Not knowing what was going to happen down the road was what was making this a great adventure.

About 150 years before we got here, prospectors and pioneers were moving into this country. What must it have been like for them to cross over the mountains and deserts hoping for a better life? I wondered how long it would have taken them to get to San Diego.

This was a good time to think about Joshua 1:9. I'm sure Joshua was concerned when he was on the east side of the Jordan River, and about to lead the Lord's people into the Promised Land. Our challenges were nothing compared to what he faced. That's when the Lord told him, *"Have I not commanded you? Be strong and courageous. Do not be frightened, and do not be dismayed, for the Lord your God is with you wherever you go."* After going over this verse in my mind for a while, I put all my worries away, and finally fell asleep leaving the night to the skunks.

We were up at the crack of dawn. Packing up the camping gear, we rode over to the Reeves' camper, and quietly deposited our big panniers in the back of Carla's pick-up. Then we headed out on the next leg of our adventure.

We started climbing as soon as we got on highway 78, but not as steeply as the stretch from Superior to Globe. The first ten miles we went from about 3500 feet above sea level to 5000 feet. This was a pleasant climb, especially without our heavy panniers. About two hours after we got on the road, Carla caught up to us. She stopped to make sure we were okay. At this point on the road, we could see the steep climb that we faced in another mile or so.

Taking a break on our way up to the pass

We had both kept the small panniers we carried on the rack over the front wheels. This day these bags held extra water, food, and bike repair stuff. I also had a bag on my handlebars containing some first aid materials, my tools, and our map. Before Carla left us heading up the road to New Mexico, Helen took the two bags off her bike, and put them in the back of Carla's truck with those we'd put in as we left the camp. Helen told me I was carrying enough for both of us, and she could get by without any bags. This was a good move, as it didn't take long for us to start the long, steep climb that would get us to the pass at 6,350 feet.

There was not much traffic on this road, although there was a highway construction crew doing some pavement patching. While it was higher than our previous climb, that experience had helped prepare us for this day. When it got too steep we were comfortable with pushing the bike on foot. Not having the panniers did make this an easier climb. Helen had been right.

As we rode over the pass and started a slight descent, we were hit with an odor. It was like the Lord had showered us with a God sized squirt of pine fragrance. What a wonderful sensation to leave the rocks and brush of the desert and mountains, and enter a beautiful pine forest on the east slope of the mountain. We stopped to breathe in the wonderful pine scent, and marvel at how fast the environment can change. The rest of our day going into New Mexico was to be mostly downhill. After inhaling the pine scent for a few minutes, we got back on the bikes and immediately had to dodge a huge rattle snake coiled in the middle of the highway. Since we were

74

riding downhill, we were past the snake almost before realizing what it was. It was one of those, "Did you see what I think I saw?" moments.

I am now ending Chapter 3 on the Arizona side of the state border, and leaving you hanging. To find out if we ever got our panniers back from Carla, and if we struck off on our own ignoring the expensive maps, you will have to read Chapter 4, *New Mexico,* one of our favorite states.

CHAPTER 4

NEW MEXICO
April 18 to May 2, 2001

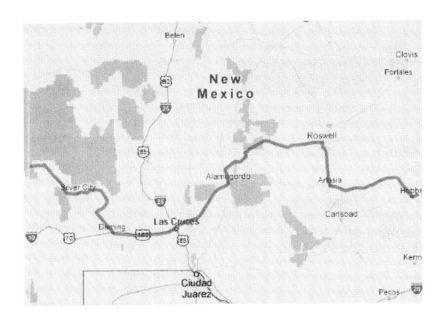

Crossing the Continental Divide

In the photo that introduces this chapter, note the lack of panniers on our bikes. Helen's looks absolutely naked. Also check out the pine trees. These were the first real trees we had encountered. This photo was taken shortly after we whizzed past the rattlesnake that was ready to spring at us.

I must have had some food in my panniers, because it wasn't long after the photo that we got to the bottom of the mountain where we found a U. S. Forest Service picnic ground alongside a babbling brook. It was very pleasant having our first meal on the road where we were sitting in a shady forest listening to water rushing over stones on its way west. Up until now, we picnicked next to dry creek beds sitting under a cactus or sage brush.

At each stop we speculated as to where our panniers might be at that particular time. If Carla was truly an angel, they were ahead of us waiting in Buckhorn at Dave and Betty Morgan's store. If she wasn't an angel, they were probably in the nearest pawnshop.

Not long after lunch, we came to Mule Creek. I had suggested to Carla that she could drop off our panniers here, since it was the first town on our map after crossing over the mountain pass. Her reaction was that it wasn't much of a town, and it would be better to drop them at Buckhorn. If anything, Carla's description of Mule Creek was an exaggeration. In fact, it wasn't a town at all. It was a post office stuck out in the wilderness. There might have been a house back behind the post office, but it wasn't very obvious. The two men standing in front told us there were no services available for us in the *town*. We took their word for it and continued on our way looking for Buckhorn, and wondering how it would compare with Mule Creek.

The rest of the afternoon was a pleasant ride in gently rolling ranch land. I would coast down a gentle slope for a half mile or so, and then try to coast as far up the next slope as possible before coasting down again. There were times I must have ridden for over a mile without having to pedal or touch my brakes.

We rode into Buckhorn about four o'clock. Compared to Mule Creek, it was a metropolis. In addition to the post office, Buckhorn had a Last Chance saloon, a café, and a trading post. There was also a sign for the Buckhorn RV Campground that seemed to be associated with the trading post. If Carla and the Morgans were on the up and up, this is where we would find our panniers.

As we walked into the trading post, we were greeted with, "Here are the cheaters!" I felt a flood of relief and emotion. Carla had indeed been our angel.

The trading post was really a general store. To our left were racks of merchandise. To the right was a counter with a coffee pot, some snacks, and a table and chairs. Sitting at the table were Pat and Mike. They were bikers following the southern tier route who had passed us the day before in Arizona. While we were camping at the Ponderosa they had camped along the road near the mountain pass, and had arrived in Buckhorn at the same time as Carla. They were waiting to see us arrive, and reclaim our panniers. Compared to them we probably were cheaters. We all had a good laugh over their comment as we sat down to compare notes on the day's ride.

Pat and Mike soon excused themselves, and headed back to the road, wanting to get some more miles in that day. For us, the day's ride was over. Betty Morgan checked us in, and we walked the bikes around to the back of the trading post to the campground. She had put us in the camp site closest to the store, so we would have easy access to the rest room. As it turned out, the only other camper that night was Ron.

Ron had been in the trading post when we arrived. He was very interested in who we were, and what we were doing. When I mentioned I liked to send an email each evening with my mailstation, but had not been able to send one the day before since I needed a phone connection, Ron offered his phone. He lives in an older, clean, and well maintained RV that was parked close to us. For the last six months, Ron had lived in Buckhorn. He explained that he works for a few years and then plays for a few years. Substitute teaching had been his work while in Buckhorn. It was about time for him to move on once he decides where he wants to go. He had just sold his horse, bought a motorcycle, and was getting restless to be on the move.

The next morning we broke camp and were ready to leave when Ron came over to say goodbye and to wish us well. It felt good to be sent off with good wishes from a fellow adventurer.

About an hour later we came to a real town; Cliff. This was a good place for breakfast at the Rambling Rose Café where we met Trish Chapman and her sister, Shawna. Shawna was our waitress and Trish was stopping on her way to work driving a van for a senior center. They gave us a lot of advice about our route to and through Texas. We found people were not reluctant to tell us which roads to take and which to avoid. The problem was roads look a lot different when you are sitting on a bicycle than when you are driving a pick-up truck or van. We listened to the advice, but didn't always believe it.

The milestone we were looking forward to that day was crossing the Continental Divide which divides the water flowing west to the Pacific Ocean from that going east to the Gulf of Mexico and the Atlantic Ocean. At 1:30 pm, Helen and I stood on the Continental Divide. That day I wrote, *"It is hard to believe we have actually propelled ourselves from the Pacific Ocean to the Continental Divide. At that moment we had a great sense of accomplishment."*

The ride up to the Divide had been a long, gradual climb. Not having to walk at all was a good feeling. We are definitely getting stronger each day. After a hug and pictures to record the event, we rode downhill into Silver City. We were now close to where we would leave the Adventure Cycling Association route map and strike out on our own.

A milestone

A Rocky Ride to City of Rocks

After three days of riding over mountain passes and crossing the Continental Divide, a third straight night sleeping in a tent didn't appeal to me. In my travels with Helen since our 1965 wedding, we have tent camped a lot and usually enjoyed the adventures that went with it. However, I never can sleep as well on the ground in a tent as I can in a bed. While camping at the Ponderosa and Buckhorn had been good experiences, we were both pleased when we got to Silver City shortly after crossing the Divide, and realized we were in a real town for a change. The prospects were good for finding a motel.

The Comfort Inn was like a palace. It was a luxury not having to set up our tent, and get out our sleeping bags. This was a good home for us for that night. In fact, after looking it

82

over, we decided this would be a good place for a rest day. Two nights it would be.

After getting settled in the Comfort Inn, we headed downtown to find a bike shop. Helen needed a new pair of cycling shorts, and I wanted to talk over our route with some bike riders.

My interest in an alternate route actually stemmed from a conversation I'd had in the fall of 2000 with two classmates from Cornell College. Bob Mead and Herman Sieck have lived in Texas for many years. At a class reunion, they made a point of getting me aside, and asking me to reconsider the route I'd told them we would be taking. The route they didn't like would take us along the Rio Grande River from El Paso. They wanted me to know that to Texans this stretch of border with Mexico was considered very dangerous. It was very remote, and had a reputation for people disappearing, being attacked, and robbed. They suggested we ride all the way across New Mexico and then enter Texas in the panhandle. This would take us on a more northern route. We could rejoin the southern tier route in east Texas.

Another friend in Florida, Victor Gallo, has ridden across the U.S. twice in bike races, and told us about the routes the races had taken. He had even shared some maps that would be of use in Texas.

East of Silver City, the southern tier route went over a mountain pass that was higher and steeper than anything we'd tackled so far. After this pass, the route turns south and follows the Rio Grande River through Las Cruzes and on down to El

Paso. I knew we could find an alternative route east from Las Cruces that would avoid our having to go into Texas until we got to the eastern border of New Mexico.

Downtown Silver City was a busy place. Helen and I were standing on a corner trying to figure out the location of the bike shop, when we were startled to hear someone say, "Frank and Helen; how are you?" Looking around, we didn't see anyone we knew. Then I spotted a cowboy grinning at us. He was wearing a western hat, boots, jeans, and a western shirt. As they would say in Hollywood, he was a cowboy right out of central casting.

This cowboy walked over laughing, saying we probably didn't recognize him dressed like that. Then we knew it was T.J.

Earlier that day, about five miles before the Continental Divide, we were overtaken by a bike rider out for a workout. He rode with us for a couple of miles as we talked about our adventure. He told us he had recently returned from riding across Australia for the second time. He has ridden all through Europe and has been across North America three times. We talked and rode until shortly before the Divide. He then wished us well, sped over the hill, and disappeared out of sight. That was T.J.

As we talked on the street, he told us that besides being a cycling nut he was also a real cowboy. I had mentioned when we were riding with him, that people (like the ladies in Cliff) always tell us to be especially careful while riding in Texas. T.J. said that people who think riding in Texas is difficult have

84

never ridden in Texas. He said, "The roads are good, and the people are friendly." That's what we wanted to hear.

T.J. also said the pass ahead of us was very difficult. Carrying our panniers would make it even more so. He suggested we find another route to Las Cruces.

When we finally found the bike shop, the people in the shop confirmed what T.J. had said. They also recommended we take a route south from Silver City to the City of Rocks State Park, and then on to Deming. From there we can ride east to Las Cruces. This route would take out mountain passes, and be a *piece of cake* for us. Their advice would have been correct if the weather hadn't gotten involved.

A day of rest was what we needed. Getting back on our bikes we felt strong. Riding east from Silver City we could turn south and go directly to the City of Rocks State Park and Deming, or we could continue east for about 20 miles and then turn south to ride along the Mimbres River before turning back west to get to the state park. Helen was pushing for the direct route south, but I was able to convince her that the better route was the one along the Mimbres River.

This longer but more interesting route took us past the Santa Rita open pit copper mine; one of the largest, if not the largest, open pit mine in the world. To say it is a huge hole in the ground is an understatement. It is gigantic. After riding a little less than an hour from Silver City we pulled to the side of the road and looked into this manmade hole. It was over a mile across and almost that deep. The trucks with ten foot diameter tires looked like little matchbox toy trucks as they crawled up out of the bottom of the pit.

Santa Rita open pit copper mine

After I'd seen enough of the pit we continued west to where we finally said goodbye to the southern tier route and turned south along the Mimbres River. This was a very pretty little river valley. The stream was not wide. Water splashing over rocks on our left and trees on our right gave this road a park like feeling as it took us gently downhill.

However, as we turned onto the road beside the river, it began to feel like we were riding with our brakes on. Even though it was downhill, there was no coasting. We had turned into a headwind that grew stronger and stronger the longer we pedaled against it. We hadn't noticed the wind before making the turn. It had been at our side or even a little behind us.

Riding into a fierce headwind is like riding uphill with no downhill payback of coasting. All we could do was shift to low gears, and keep the pedals moving.

We left Silver City at seven that morning. At one in the afternoon we were sitting on the porch of the Faywood post office/general store. We needed a break! In the five hours we'd been on the road, we'd covered just 40 miles. Usually we had been averaging between 13 and 15 miles per hour. Today it averaged out to 8 miles per hour, and 26 miles of that had been with the wind. I was ready to throw in the towel. Our goal was now the City of Rocks rather than Deming. We had just 8 more miles to go.

The last 8 miles took an hour and a half. The first four miles was still into the wind. We thought we'd get some relief when we turned to the west for the last 4 miles to our destination. However, the situation went from bad to worse. The wind was howling from the south, and with our panniers on the bikes, we had become a moving barrier for the wind to push against. Gusts of wind actually blew us off the road. We never fell, but several times when we were hit by a gust, we stopped, got off the bikes, and just held on for dear life to keep everything upright.

When we turned into the gate for City of Rocks State Park, we finally felt like we had won the battle. With the wind at our back, we sprinted the half mile to the park entrance and campground check-in.

The park ranger empathized with our struggle getting there. He said the winds had gusted to 60 miles per hour just before we arrived. Those were the gusts that made us dismount and hold on for dear life. To give us some relief from the wind, he assigned us to a camp site where we would be sheltered on the south and west by huge rocks.

That evening we set up camp in the lee of the rocks and had a pleasant view across a valley as we ate our dinner and talked over this most difficult of biking days. Off in the valley, we watched a dust storm roll over the desert with a wall of sand pouring north toward Silver City. We thanked the Lord we were safe, and out of the way of more trouble.

Our camp in City of Rocks State Park

The wind had pretty much died down as we went to bed inside our tent. Around midnight, we were awakened by the wind howling again. This time it was coming from the north. We were no longer in the lee of the rocks. Now we were totally exposed to a wind that seemed to want to tear us lose from the ground, and set us rolling around the campground inside the tent. Again we were hanging on for dear life. The tent was flapping and cracking. On top of that, the temperature, which had been warm all day, plummeted to freezing. Our sleeping bags were rated for 40 degrees, and it was a lot colder than that. All we could do was put on every bit of clothes we had with us in the tent, and hang on until the sun came up.

The night finally ended, and we crawled out of the tent to survey the damage. All of our equipment was intact. We hurriedly packed, and rode to the camp restroom where there was shelter and some heat. It was crowded with other campers. We weren't the only ones who had been suffering all night.

We warmed up, and compared notes with the other campers before heading out for Deming. With the cold north wind at our back, the 30 miles to Deming was covered in less than two hours. We located a motel and went to check in hoping to get back to bed, and finish our night's sleep that had been so rudely interrupted by the cold and wind.

We had arrived too early to get a room. They were all occupied, and we wouldn't be able to move in for another hour. After breakfast at a Denny's restaurant, we returned to the motel, and got to bed. We woke up just in time for the Sunday evening worship service at the church across the street. Then it was back to bed for a good night's sleep in preparation for the 65 miles we needed to ride tomorrow if we were to get to Las Cruces. There is nothing between Deming and Las Cruces, so we had no options but to go all the way regardless of the weather or riding conditions.

As I finally got to bed that night, I was wondering if maybe the high mountain pass we had avoided would have been easier than the 60 mile an hour winds. That's something I'll never know.

Two Milestones

When we had settled on a new route through New Mexico, I noted that it would take us through Roswell. My cousin, Mary Glen Reeves, lives there. I had visited her family in 1964 as I was on my way home after a trip to Mexico where I met Helen and fell in love. When I contacted Mary Glen to let her know we'd be riding through Roswell, she told me she and her husband, Mike, would be traveling through Las Cruces while we were there. They were going to Tucson to see a son, and would be back in Roswell the next week end. Plans were made for us to meet in Las Cruces, and then again the next Sunday in Roswell where we'd go to their church.

It was fun to see this cousin after all these years and to catch up on our families. They also gave us a little tour around Las Cruces. The route they took from Roswell to Las Cruces was the same route we'd be taking east. There was a mountain pass we'd be riding over not many miles to our east. When I asked how difficult it would be on a bicycle, Mike said it shouldn't be hard to ride. He had no trouble in his car. I, on the other hand, was not convinced, and asked if he'd drive us out to see San Agustin Pass. After seeing it myself, I had to agree with him. It didn't look that difficult.

The next morning, we were riding up to the top of this pass, and my opinion changed; *BIG TIME!*

As we approached the summit, the wind was being funneled right into our faces. It was almost like the ride to City of Rocks all over again. Once we had to dismount from the bikes to keep from being blown off the mountain, no way could we get back on the bikes with enough momentum to even stay on them let alone pedal on to the top. We actually had to push the last couple of hundred yards.

Resting on a rock beside the highway, the view from San Agustin Pass was worth the effort. Before us was the Tularosa Basin that seemed to go forever. In the prairie to our right was a herd of horses that we took to be wild. Usually horses we had seen were near a ranch house or in a corral. These were roaming the range with no sign of human habitation anywhere near. The horses seemed to be as curious about us as we were about them. However, as we tried to approach, they would have none of that, and moved away. They then disappeared over a slight rise.

The ride down the east side of the pass was a great payback time as we felt like we were flying on a wide open road. After several miles, we could look back to where we had been, and it became obvious why these were called the Organ Mountains. From the east, they looked a lot like a church pipe organ.

I was looking forward to visiting the White Sands National Monument on the road we'd be taking through this basin. The

White Sands are gypsum sand that resembles snow. In fact, in places there were sand drifts that had been plowed to keep the road clear. We stopped at the Visitor's Center, where we were greeted by name by another visitor. We had met Stephen in Las Cruces. He had told us stories about his experience riding a bike across the country in the 80's. His purpose for being in New Mexico was to explore a canyon where there were a lot of migrating humming birds. Stephen said he thought he might be seeing us this day at the White Sands. When I asked about the humming birds, he laughed, and said he'd found the canyon, saw a Monarch butterfly, and a picture of a humming bird. I guess he'd missed the migration

After we had met Stephen in Las Cruces, Helen and I had talked about the older people we had met who were doing interesting and exciting things during their retirement years. A couple back in the City of Rocks were hiking all through the west looking for evidence of the Immigrant Trail that had been taken by people going to California during the Gold Rush. They were mapping the trail as well as collecting artifacts they found at old camp sites.

. In Deming, at the motel where we were staying, we met a man who was returning home from a motorcycle ride to the southern tip of South America. That adventure put our little bike ride to shame.

92

In the White Sands National Monument

Riding out of the basin on the east side, we had a long uphill ride through the Mescalero Apache Indian Reservation. These were some serious mountains. Our goal was the city of Ruidoso, which was about 120 miles from Las Cruces. We had stopped half-way in Alamogordo shortly after the White Sands, and were now attacking another range of mountains.

We had mentioned to people that our goal for the day was Ruidoso, and the reaction was, "that's a resort town." After the experiences we had getting this far into New Mexico, a resort town appealed to us. First we had to get over these mountains.

The ride up to Apache Summit was not as steep as others had been, and we were not bothered by the wind. Most of it was in a beautiful pine forest. There was no walking! We felt strong as we reached Apache Summit at 7591 feet. This was a milestone. It was the highest elevation on our cross-continent ride. It was a wonderful feeling of accomplishment as we congratulated each other on making this climb on our bikes with absolutely no hiking this day. It turned out this also was our last mountain pass. There were still many hills, some steep, ahead of us, but none of them would be climbs miles long.

Another milestone

The second milestone was when we rode into Ruidoso, and our total miles passed 1000. What a day this was! Our highest point and then to realize that with our own legs we had covered a thousand miles. We were ready to enjoy a tourist town.

When we were checking in at the Comfort Inn in downtown Ruidoso, Helen mentioned we had bikes, and would like a room on the ground floor if possible. Upon hearing what Helen had said, the manager came out of his office. Some other guests who checked in earlier had told him they had seen a couple on bikers riding up to Apache Summit. He was hoping we'd stop at the Comfort Inn so he could meet us, and hear about our trip. Then he turned to the clerk registering us, and told him to upgrade us to the first floor suite, the best room in the Inn. We felt special. In fact, we felt so special we stayed for two nights.

I mentioned there were no more mountains for us to climb. Leaving Ruidoso we left the mountains behind and found all the hills ahead to be a *piece of cake*. Helen insisted on our taking the Southern Tier Route to avoid the mountains further to our north. What we had was enough of a challenge for a couple who had trained for hills by riding over the Sebastian Inlet Bridge on highway A1A.

One other hill of note was in eastern New Mexico on our last full day in this state. Between Artesia and Lovington, we were riding through the first oil field we'd seen. In fact, it was the first time I'd seen an oil drilling rig. The ride that day was mostly uphill as we were riding out of the Pecos River Valley. Then, instead of a gradual uphill, it got a lot steeper and we climbed a substantial height. At the top, I was looking for the payback downhill glide, but there was no downhill. We found ourselves on a flat plain. The payback didn't come until we were in Texas a couple of days later. As I've thought about it since that day, I think the climb took us to the Caprock which is a mesa that straddles the New Mexico – Texas border. I had driven down it west of Amarillo several years before and marveled at how the land just seems to drop away at the edge of this mesa. This really was our last BIG hill.

Our last night in New Mexico was in Lovington. I closed my email journal that night with these words:

"Lord willing, this will be our last night in New Mexico. I don't know if it is because their governor, Gary Johnson, is a bike rider, or if it's just that they are naturally friendly, but New Mexico has treated us very well. The roads have been excellent for the most part, and from Carla who carried our bags to Buckhorn, to Cliff who gave us a ride to the supermarket yesterday in Artesia, we have been treated royally. They call their state the Land of Enchantment. We have found that to be true. Now we are headed to Texas, and wondering how they can top New Mexico."

That last evening in New Mexico, Helen announced her goal was to ride all the way home without having one flat tire. The next morning, by the dawn's early light, I was sitting by the highway, still in New Mexico, fixing Helen's flat rear tire. I'm sorry she didn't reach this goal. It would have saved me a little work.

Billy the Kid

I've seen a lot of signs announcing HISTORIC MARKER AHEAD as I drive down the highway. "What could be historic out here in the middle of nowhere?" is my usual thought as I roar on past in the car. I've become suspicious of the use of the word *historic*. In my dictionary this word is defined *famous or important in history or likely to be seen as such in the future* (*Oxford Dictionary of Current English*). In Florida, about every town over 50 years of age announces its HISTORIC DOWNTOWN. Does every downtown fit the description? Maybe I'm an old *fuddy duddy*, but it seems that at this time the definition might be changed to *anything anyone calls historic.*

With that mind set, I'm inclined to not stop out in the wide open spaces to read the markers. However, it all changes when I'm on a bike pedaling through these wide open spaces looking for any excuse to stop, get off the bike saddle, and have a drink of water. In New Mexico, we found a number of interesting historic markers, and almost all of them had to do with Billy the Kid.

Stopping to read the markers, we learned a lot about this famous, historic figure from the Wild West. We learned that the historians don't know for certain what his last name was. His first name was Billy, no doubt about that. The name we know him by, *Billy the Kid*, is partly because of the confusion about his last name, and the fact that he was young. As an orphan, he grew up in Silver City, and was described as a hard working, honest boy by the family that took him in. His first run in with the law was after being accused of murdering a man who had taunted and threatened him. He was probably defending himself when he killed this person. Billy was put in jail to await his trial, but soon escaped by climbing up the inside of a chimney. From that time on (he was probably about 16 at the time); Billy was seen as an outlaw. He worked for a while as a cowboy in Arizona and then headed toward Lincoln County, New Mexico, where Ruidoso is located.

Billy had become very skilled with guns, and was usually carrying both a rifle and revolver. Gunslingers could find work in Lincoln County because of what has become known as the Lincoln County War.

The two warring parties were trying to get control of the county, and each had a small army of gunmen to do their fighting. Billy signed on with one side, but one of the historic markers explained that when he had the opportunity to meet the leader of the other side, he liked him more than his current boss, so he changed sides. Billy certainly killed people in this war, but the historians don't think it was the large number that has been credited to him.

When Billy shot and killed the sheriff of Lincoln County, he became an even more wanted man. Many of the Historic Markers were identifying his hide outs. He must have spent a lot of time hiding.

The most interesting marker was on a building in the old, historic part of Las Cruces. Before it was Las Cruces, the city was named Mesilla. My cousin Mary Glen and her husband, Mike, took us down to the Old Mesilla Plaza for lunch, and there on the side of a building was a large Historic Marker indicating that this building was where Billy the Kid was tried, and sentenced to be hung. Before they could hang him, he again escaped. Pat Garrett was the law in that part of the country, and he hunted down Billy. Eventually he shot, and killed him.

In death, Billy the Kid has become a famous folk hero. You get the idea riding these roads that Billy the Kid is the most famous person from that area. Riding along with these Historic

Markers made me feel like I was really in what had been the Wild West.

Helen is with Billy the Kid in Old Mesilla Plaza in Las Cruces.

Dogs

The books I read in preparation for this bike adventure all had a section advising how to cope with the aggressive dogs we were bound to encounter. The most common advice was based on the belief dogs chased bicycles because the revolving pedal action excited them, and made them want a piece of the rider. All the authors had had experience with dogs, and shared the avoidance method that seemed most effective for them. A young man in a bike shop here in Florida even told me an experience he had when a dog came after him. This dog bit at his foot. He missed the foot, but tore the pedal from his bike. I didn't really believe that story, but I also didn't know the dog.

The most common advice from the veteran riders was to stop, and walk your bike past the dog. Their theory is the dog will lose his motivation when the pedal stops revolving. Stopping in front of a growling, menacing dog didn't always seem like a smart thing to do. It would really break up the rhythm of the ride to stop frequently, and what if this dog didn't know he was supposed to stop when I did.

The dogs we encountered along our route were territorial. Each one had been assigned a section of the road to protect, and it was their job to harass any bike riders coming into their assigned section. When we left his area, the dog would trot back to his home, and lay down waiting for the next trespasser.

These dogs didn't seem to be distance runners. In fact, they seemed to be quite lazy. A quick burst of speed on our part, and the chase was over. They seemed to know the sooner they gave up the chase, the closer they would be to their usual lookout and resting spot.

In New Mexico, we had two memorable dog encounters worth reporting. The first was on the ride up to Apache Summit on our way from Alamogordo to Ruidoso. Unlike the rest of New Mexico, in the Apache Reservation, the houses are very close to the road. As we approached one house shortly after beginning our climb, I noticed three dogs eyeing us from beside this house. Climbing up this steep grade to our highest point on the entire cross-continent ride meant we were not moving fast. The chance to put on a burst of speed was very slight if these dogs became aggressive. I followed Helen, keeping watch on the dogs. The house was only about five yards off the road. If these dogs became aggressive, there wouldn't be time to prepare for their attack. In just a couple of doggy leaps, they would be on us.

Helen was almost past the house when one dog, obviously the alpha male, came charging out at me. I decided to try a new tactic. Unfortunately I had not briefed Helen on this new strategy. Since a burst of speed was out of the question, talking to the dog might work. After all, dogs are used to hearing human voices and following commands. Helen thought I only talked to her. Looking back at the charging mongrel I shouted, "STOP!" When Helen heard me shout stop, she did. I was looking back at the dog to see if he was going to mind my command. Helen just had put her foot on the ground when I plowed into the back of her bike. We both fell on our left side under the fully loaded bikes.

Lying under my bike, waiting for the dog to pounce on my throat, I looked up in amazement as Helen, crawling out from under her bike, sprang to her feet, and in no time had her finger pointing at the beast. "Bad dog, bad dog," she informed him. "In fact" she continued, "you are one of the worst examples of dog I've ever seen. You should be ashamed of yourself. Don't you see what you have done?" The ferocious little dog had stopped in his tracts when we fell. Now he stood wagging his tail, listening to Helen insult him, and his ancestors. Her lecture continued until the tail went from wagging to being tucked between his hind legs. Finally he slinked back to his

101

companions who had observed all this from near the house. With their mouths open, and their tails also tucked, they appeared to be amazed their alpha male had been totally humiliated, and intimidated by this grey haired alpha female. I must admit lying on the ground under our bikes watching, and listening to Helen, I was also impressed as well as humbled by my alpha female partner.

After venting her anger at this poor dog, Helen came back to help me, and the bikes back up. We sat by the side of the road as we cleaned the scratches, and put on bandages. Neither of us was hurt, but we did have some bleeding cuts that we attended to before getting back on the road. For Helen, who had fallen, and hit her head back in Arizona, this fall was nothing. I, on the other hand, lacked falling experience, and was a little more shaken up.

When we finally figured out what had happened, and why Helen had stopped, we had a good laugh. Getting back on the bikes and preparing to continue our climb up to the summit, we glanced back at our attackers. The three dogs were all peeking around a tree watching us. I do believe they were sorry for what they had done, and we forgave them as we rode on up the mountain.

The rest of the day's ride to Ruidoso, I had blood trickling down my leg. Helen gave me no sympathy. My little "boo-boo" as she called it, wasn't enough to warrant sympathy. Her attitude was for me to take it like a man, and keep pedaling. Sometimes it can be tough riding with an alpha female, especially if you're looking for pity.

Looking for some sympathy

The other memorable incident took place at the beginning of our last full day in New Mexico. We were riding out of Artesia and the Pecos River Valley before sunrise. After our experiences with the wind back at the City of Rocks, we had concluded getting an early start would get us to our destination for the day before the wind found us. Speaking of our daily destination, most days we didn't have a destination before we got on the road. After riding about six hours, if we were near a town with a motel, and we felt like stopping, we did. If the next town was close, we might go on, but we weren't in a big rush to finish the adventure.

It was dark as we pedaled down the road that would take us out of Artesia. Passing a junk yard, we could hear a ferocious dog running alongside us behind a fence. We could barely make out the dog in the dim light, but he looked and sounded big. The growling and barking was what you would expect from an ugly *junk yard dog.* I was feeling pretty cocky with the fence between us, and started to talk to the dog while Helen was trying to get as far ahead of me as possible. My comments could have been interpreted as taunting. I pointed out things about his genealogy and his lack of beauty. He surely couldn't understand what I was saying, but it did seem to make him even more eager to come out to take a bite out of me. I was laughing at his frustration when he gave a lunge into the fence. To my shock and horror, the fence broke open from the force of his jump. I yelled to Helen, "He's out of the fence!" With the motivation of my not wanting to have a close and personal interaction with this brute, I put on a burst of speed that even surprised me. We were now in a desperate race with this dog. Thank the Lord, we won. Adrenaline is a great thing when you need it. Perhaps the dog lost interest when he thought about his having abandoned his post in the junk yard. Whatever his reason, he broke off the chase at the edge of town. We didn't go back to make sure he returned safely to his junk yard.

The next day we entered Texas. There were dogs in Texas as well, but you will have to wait for the next chapter to read about them. Needless to say, there will be no photos of dogs. We weren't foolish enough to stop and pose with any of them, although the three in the Indian Reservation would have made a cute picture.

I need to rest before going into Texas

CHAPTER 5

TEXAS
MAY 2 to MAY 20

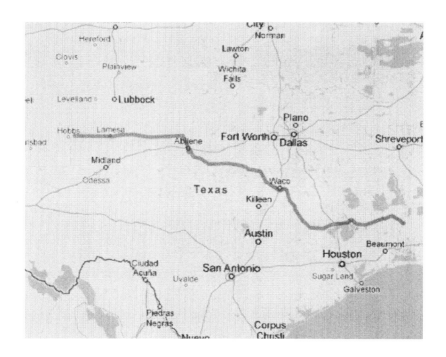

Our First Texas Angel

Texas had become almost a mythical place in my mind. Perhaps it was because so many people along our bike route had warned us about riding there, or perhaps because it would be almost a third of our cross-continent distance, or maybe it was because of all the western movies I'd watched, or maybe it was because I'd never traveled through the state and was wondering what lay ahead. Whatever the reason, we were happy to get there, and looking forward to a Texas experience.

As a freshman in 1956 at Cornell College in Iowa, I'd become friends with Herman Sieck and Bob Mead. During our sophomore year we joined the Owls social group along with several other great guys. Over the years we have remained friends, and while we lost contact for several years, in 2000 we had reconnected. Herman now lived near Houston and Bob was living in San Antonio. These were the two that strongly advised us to take a route through Texas that was not right along the Mexican border.

Following Herm's and Bob's advice, we entered Texas in the south part of the panhandle on highway 180 from Hobbs, New Mexico. Herm had told me he would have people looking out for us as soon as we crossed the border. I thought he was kidding, but he wasn't.

Our last night in New Mexico, we received a call on our cell phone. The person calling identified himself as Dick Knittle; a friend of Herm Sieck's who lived in Midland, Texas. He was intrigued by our adventure, and had been reading my daily email journal Herm was posting on the Owls' website.

108

Dick and his wife, Norma, wanted to meet us. We agreed to make our second stop in Texas at the town of Lamesa. Dick and Norma would drive up to give us our official Texas welcome.

The next day, on our way to Texas, Helen had her flat tire. I had packed what I thought would be enough tire tubes to last for the entire trip. After repairing Helen's flat I inventoried my supply, and found we were down to four tubes. With four tires on the pavement at all times, four tubes in reserve could go in a hurry if we ran into an especially rough stretch of road.

In his book *All the Way to Lincoln Way,* Bill Roe recounted an experience we wanted to avoid. Riding through rural Iowa he had a flat tire, and did not have a spare. His wife was driving a support vehicle, and would meet him at prearranged points each day. He carried a cell phone in case of an emergency. At the spot he had his flat there was no cell phone service. Bill's wife had driven on ahead to meet family at the place where his ride would end that day. Bill sat on the side of the road for a long time. Finally the family became concerned when he hadn't shown up. Back tracking on his route, they found Bill waiting to be rescued. I didn't want this to happen to us, so we needed four more tubes.

Most of the small towns we were riding through didn't have bike shops selling the tube size we needed. Dick Knittle sounded happy to be able to help, and was sure he could find a bike shop in Midland. I gave him the tube size we needed.

The next day, Dick and Norma had the honor of being our first Texas angels. They not only brought the tubes to Lamesa, but took us to lunch. Dick told us stories about when he and Herm worked together in what Texans call the "Oil Patch."

The meal with Dick and Norma in Lamesa was a special treat. Our first day in Texas had not been a good one for Helen. She doesn't eat meat, but will eat fish. In our first overnight stop at the town of Seminole, Helen had inquired at our motel where we would be able to find a seafood dinner. After thinking about this request for what seemed like a long time, the motel manager directed us to a restaurant on the highway north of town.

At dinner time, we got on our bikes, and rode through town looking for this *seafood restaurant*. We finally found it in a gas station. It was a convenience store with a little buffet set-up. After looking over the buffet, Helen finally identified what must have been what they were calling fish. She put some on her plate, and sat with me at the table. Helen was really hungry for fish. I couldn't remember the last time she ate anything that was fried, let alone fried fish. She craved fish so much that she was willing to overlook the fried part of this meal. As she started to cut the fish with her knife, it wouldn't cut. It was like a board. She said it was so hard she could pound a nail with it.

Helen walked up to the person who seemed to be keeping the buffet supplied, and complained that she couldn't eat the fish. "Oh, I'm sorry," he said. "I guess this has been on the buffet for a while, I'll get you some that is fresher." He disappeared into what must have been the kitchen, quickly reappearing with a plate, and Helen's new piece of fried fish.

110

Helen stabbed the fish with her fork to get a good grip on it so as to cut a bite, and the fork bounced off the fish. At this point, she learned that in Texas, seafood could mean crispy fried fish (or whatever it was). She did chew on a little of the fried fish, and then gave up. While this was going on, I was enjoying my hamburger.

Several days later we rode past a restaurant that had a sign out front, "Crispiest Fried Fish in Texas." We took their word for it.

The Abilene Angel

Helen and I were watching the weather reports on TV after Dick and Norma left us in Lamesa. The last couple of days we had been dogged by a weather front, and from the TV reports, the front had caught us. We were now sitting in a tornado watch area with thunderstorms forecast for the following day. Our previous rest days had been in interesting places like Silver City and Ruidoso. Lamesa wasn't like these *touristy* stop over's, but riding in a thunderstorm didn't appeal to either of us. The decision was to stay put for a day, and get on the sunny side of the weather.

We didn't have to get out early to avoid the wind on this rest day, so sleeping in was in order. When we finally got up, I was shocked when I saw Helen's right eye. It was very red and swollen. Something was wrong, and it could be serious. I insisted that we find a doctor in Lamesa to get whatever treatment she needed to heal this ugly looking eye. It was strange that we hadn't noticed anything the day before. Evidently something was wrong long before this, but now was the time it got bad enough to be noticeable.

Looking in the Lamesa phone directory, we found a walk-in clinic. The people in the motel gave us directions to the clinic. We got on our bikes, and headed toward where we had been directed. This was not a fun ride. While the decision to make this a rest day was a good one, trying to ride the short distance to the clinic was challenging. We were pelted by rain as we splashed along. The streets were flooded. Lightning and thunder were crackling all around us. This actually was another courageous ride.

When Helen came back into the waiting room where I had stayed while she was being treated, she was soaking wet, and not a happy camper. Her first comment was that she doubted this man was a real doctor. He had spilled solution all over her while trying to flush her eye. "All the time," she said, "he was talking about when he had lived in Florida, and wishing he was still there." I had to wonder why anyone would leave Florida for Lamesa. The thought went through my mind that perhaps he was in the government witness protection program.

From the doctor's office, we got back on the bikes, and searched for a pharmacy where we could get a prescription filled. The rain was still coming down. The only good thing was we'd been carrying rain gear with us for almost 1300 miles, and were finally getting a chance to use it.

The afternoon was spent in the motel room where we treated Helen's eye. She obviously had an infection. Something had gotten in her eye to cause this infection. The only thing we could think of was the strong, *blow you off the bike*, wind between Silver City and City of Rocks. That had been almost two weeks before, but maybe it took that long for this infection to get this bad.

The next morning we tried to be optimistic and think her eye was better, but it wasn't. We made the decision to get back on the road for a 70 mile ride to Snyder. If her eye didn't improve, Lamesa wasn't the place we wanted to be.

This was actually one of the days I remember fondly. Fifteen miles into the ride, we had payback for the long climb last Tuesday to the top of the Caprock between Artesia and Lovington, New Mexico. As we coasted off the Caprock the land changed from cotton farms to range land. The bottom of the rock was in Borden County. The only town in this county is Gail with a population of 200. Needless to say, unlike most county seats, there was no courthouse square in Gail. From my days as a mathematics teacher, I knew you would need more than one street to make a square.

There was a sign near the courthouse with this quote by Gail Borden. "I tried and failed. So I tried and tried and then I succeeded." This wasn't a bad message to get as we looked for another doctor. I had never heard of Gail Borden, but have done a Google search and found several libraries with that name. I think he was the founder of the Borden's Dairy.

We stopped at the Coyote Café in Gail. This might have been the only café and store in the county. There were several small tables with chairs in the front. One table had about a half dozen men sitting around having a cup of coffee, and discussing the weather and other things that ranchers, farmers, and small town people talk about. They were friendly, and didn't tease us about our funny clothes.

It became clear we weren't going to be waited on sitting at a table, so we walked over to the lady who was the cook, as well as the store manager. This was also the gas station, so she kept busy. After placing a breakfast order, I walked around and picked up a bottle of orange juice. I mentioned to the lady that I'd gotten it. Her reply was, "That's okay, I just watch what people take, and figure it all in at the end." The men all laughed, and warned me that what she really does is weigh everyone before they leave.

Borden County Courthouse, Gail, Texas

This sort of broke the ice, and I started to ask questions about the town and county. I'd noticed a school as we rode off the Caprock and into town. They told me that was the only

114

school in Borden County. Some children rode a total of 150 miles a day on the school bus. They also let me know that the football stadium could seat more than the total county population. I'll bet this place rocks on fall Friday nights.

We finished our ride that day in Snyder. Helen's eye was no better after a day of treatment. This concerned us. Studying our map, I searched for the nearest town that would be large enough to have an ophthalmologist. We were about a hundred miles west and north of Abilene. Surely this city would have a bona fide eye doctor who could properly treat Helen's eye. The next day was Sunday. We'd miss church that day, and ride to Anson, a little over 60 miles from Snyder. Our plan was to ride south to Abilene Monday morning, and spend the day looking for an eye doctor. We could have ridden on to Abilene, but we both had a feeling that Anson should be our goal for that day.

Arriving in Anson before noon, we stopped at a motel. They were in the process of cleaning the rooms. We were told we could have one, but we needed to come back after 2 o'clock. This arrangement satisfied us since we were just killing time until we'd get to Abilene in the morning.

I'd read about a mural that had been painted in the Anson post office during the Great Depression. The government at that time had hired artists to paint murals in public buildings. The one in the Anson post office was named, "Cowboys Dancing." We found the post office, and the lobby was open this Sunday morning. Looking past the lobby, I could get a view of the mural. While it depicted cowboys dancing, it wasn't worth a special trip to Anson.

115

The downtown of Anson was very dead the day we visited. Many buildings were boarded up. On one side of the square was a large building that I could imagine was a beautiful opera house about a hundred years ago.

Our tour of Anson ended at a Laundromat across from the motel. Helen had decided to take advantage of this time to get some laundry done. Most of our clothes were the kind that we could wash at night in our room, but it was nice to get some things washed with a real washer and dryer.

On the square in Anson

While the laundry machines were doing their thing with our clothes, we walked next door to the local Dairy Queen. This

116

was the only eating place we had seen during our bike tour of Anson. Most of the people in the DQ were dressed like they had just come from church. We got a lot of sideways looks because of our different appearance, but no one said a word to us. I was afraid someone could get a whip lash in his neck from turning his head so fast to not let me see him staring.

Sitting in a booth across from us was a couple with an older gentleman. I had noticed them inspecting us, but they hadn't asked the usual questions, "Who are you and where are you going?" Curiosity finally got the best of the younger man. As they were starting to leave, he asked the questions. This followed with our telling stories, and his telling about one summer in college when he had ridden a bike from Maine to Abilene. It was fun talking to another person who had experienced an adventure similar to ours.

We had all said our goodbyes when he turned back to us asking where we were going from Anson. I told him our plans for going to Abilene in the morning to find an eye doctor. His eyes got big, and he gave his wife a knowing smile. Then he took out his business card, and wrote something on it. Handing me the card, he said, "This is the name of the best eye doctor in Abilene, and this is his phone number. He was my college roommate. You call this number, and tell them you have an emergency. I know he'll see you as soon as possible." With that he walked out of the DQ.

All I know about this man is that his name is Rick Lewis. He was with his wife and father driving through Anson, and stopped for lunch in the Dairy Queen. I had to wonder about the

117

doctor who had been his roommate in college. How likely was it that the only person we talked to in Anson not only knew the best eye doctor in Abilene, but also had the phone number in his memory? I remembered my verse for this trip and how the Lord tells us in Joshua 1:9 that He is with us wherever we go. Was this a Texas angel? The answer to my skepticism would come the next day.

The road south from Anson to Abilene became an expressway as we approached the city. Getting off on one of the first exits, we stopped at a McDonald's for breakfast. I was waiting until about nine o'clock to call the doctor, figuring that would be the time the office would open, if, in fact, I actually had the number of a doctor's office.

I finally called the number. A doctor's receptionist answered my call. When I explained my purpose in calling, she explained the doctor I was asking for was in surgery that morning, but there would be another doctor who could see Helen. She told us to come to the office, and they'd fit Helen in. I told her we were unfamiliar with the city, and I needed directions. I might not have mentioned that we were riding bikes. The directions she gave were for us to get on the expressway, and take it around to the south side of the city. We'd find their office on the street just past the hospital.

Without much hesitation, we got on the expressway riding south. As with all interstates and expressways, we found a good riding shoulder. Following her directions, we had no trouble finding the hospital and the eye clinic.

118

Helen went in to the clinic while I stayed out to secure our bikes. I also made a phone call to Herm Sieck. We were making plans to meet Herm and his wife, Suzi, and Bob and Barbara Mead in a few days in Waco, Lord willing.

Having finished my business outside, I walked into the clinic to wait with Helen. She wasn't there. The waiting room was packed, but no Helen. I was hoping she had already gone in to see the doctor, so I sat in the one empty chair, and looked at all the patients who were staring without making eye contact at this strange looking man who had just joined them wearing tight biking shorts and a neon yellow jersey.

A few minutes after I sat down, I heard Helen's voice. She was coming down the hall toward me with two nurses and a man in a suit. They were all asking her about her adventure and giving her the VIP treatment. You would have thought they were all old friends. After hugs all around, she walked over to me. The man who had walked out with Helen and the nurses was very interested in her story. He walked over, and asked if he could see the prescription. He looked at it before walking out the door ahead of us. In answer to my question about who he was, Helen said she had no idea.

As we were getting our bikes unlocked, and Helen was telling me what the doctor had said, the man returned with a box. "Here is a whole box of the eye drops on your prescription. You don't want to have to go to a pharmacy with your eyes dilated. I'm a rep for the drug company, and we'd like to just give this to you." With that, he walked away leaving us holding the box of eye drops, and trying to figure out how to get them in our packed panniers.

The prescription Helen had gotten in Lamesa was not what she needed. Her eye healed fast with the new eye drops given by the pharmacy representative. We actually ended our ride in Florida with most of the box of drops still packed in my pannier.

As we reflected on the experience in Anson with Rick, we were sure that the Lord had sent Rick there for us. He was just passing through the town, and was likely the only person in Anson at that time that had the doctor's name and phone number memorized. The treatment at the clinic was so reassuring. We knew the Lord was in this, and rode on east the next day wondering what He had planned as our next surprise. You'll have to wait to read about that, because it is now time to tell some Texas dog stories.

Texas Dogs

Dogs seemed to be everywhere in Texas. My overall impression was that most of them were much closer to the ugly end of the scale than to the cute end. I suspect that at some time there had been a contest to see who could breed the ugliest dog in Texas. It must have been very competitive.

Besides physical appearance, another quality shared by most of the dogs was laziness. (I'm generalizing here so any Texas dog owners who read this can believe their animal is the exception.) Most of them didn't have either the staying power or the motivation of the junk yard dog in Artesia, New Mexico.

In order to give these lazy dogs some needed physical activity, I tried to adjust my speed to stay just a few feet ahead of the brute. My hope was that as long as he believed he was close enough to catch me, he'd keep running for a longer distance. I had fun playing like the carrot on the stick, encouraging him to keep trying. Helen didn't really appreciate this strategy. This was especially true when she was following me. I had to promise that I'd only try the dog physical improvement program when she was in the lead. Having a large dog's breath warming the back of her leg wasn't a feeling she enjoyed.

In our predawn departures from the little towns, I liked to think of the dogs as cheerleaders encouraging us, and wishing us a good day on the road.

The second stop after Abilene was the town of Dublin. Dublin was the home of Dr. Pepper. We had the opportunity to visit the soda fountain where Dr. Pepper had introduced his beverage. The original tasted better to me than the modern version, but both are good.

My journal entry for the day we left Dublin included this:

The dogs of Dublin were cheering for us as we rode out of town in the dark at five this morning. Well, I think it could have been cheering. It seemed that every dog in town joined in the chorus. We couldn't see them, but from the variety of dog voices, I could imagine the little, bouncing, yipping terriers as the tenors, and the ugly, steroid-taking, shaggy brutes as the basses with the spaniels, hounds, and other mongrels filling in the second tenor and baritone parts.

Dublin, Texas

Along the route today, we passed through the town of Hico. Besides their Cowboy Hall of Fame, they also have a Billy the Kid museum. Helen and I went through Hico before the museums opened, so we'll just have to wonder what Billy the Kid was doing in this part of Texas. I thought we had left him dead at the hands of Sheriff Pat Garrett back in New Mexico.

Between Dublin and Meridian, the end of our day's ride, we did have some dog excitement. We were riding over a railroad overpass. In this flat and empty country, you could see for long distances from the top of an overpass. As I scanned the railroad tracks below us, I noticed a pack of six to eight dogs emerging from a grove of trees about a quarter mile from the road. My first reaction was to figure out the extent of their territory, so as to plan how I'd deal with them if they came after us. Looking into the distance in all directions, I didn't see a house. I then realized these were wild dogs with no territorial boundary.

Three miles ahead, we could see a crossroads with what was probably a gas station or truck stop. I called to Helen to make her aware of the dogs, and that we'd probably have to out run them to the crossroads.

The ride down the overpass gave us a good head of steam. I hoped the dogs would ignore us. Our speed off the overpass got their attention. They stopped about a hundred yards to our left to watch and I commented on how they didn't seem to want to get in a race. Then one of them, evidently the alpha male, gave a deep bark and started towards us. Actually he was aiming in front of us in an attempt to cut us off. He had every intention to get a bite out of us and perhaps dinner. We probably were going to be the breakfast that would replace the deer or whatever it was they had been hunting in the grove of trees.

The only action we could take was to ride as fast as we could toward the crossroads hoping we could out run this pack of dogs, or tire them out so they would give up, and look for an easier prey. As I've written before, adrenaline is a great thing when you are under attack. I think we were both surprised we could ride at a sprinting speed for as far as we did. Every time I looked back, the dogs were still chasing.

123

It wasn't until we were almost to the crossroads that they broke off the chase. We coasted into the gas station/convenience store feeling like we had just outrun a great danger. The few people in the store were totally clueless that these two bikers had just escaped from a pack of hungry brutes. We were totally exhilarated, and they were totally clueless. We were congratulating each other and hugging, and they were acting as if, like them, we'd just driven a pick-up truck in for gas.

The following day, May 11, we were approaching Waco from the north on a nice country highway (Texas highway 6) with a good shoulder and light traffic. As we got closer to Waco the traffic started to increase and then the two lane road became a four lane divided highway. Riding on the shoulder of this expressway was like riding on a bike trail. We were making good time and enjoying the ride when suddenly the shoulder went away. We were standing at a bridge over Lake Waco. At the south end of the bridge, over a mile away, we could see the city. The traffic had been building as we approached Waco, and was now quite heavy. Standing at the end of the bridge, we assessed our options.

It didn't take us long to realize that if we were to get to Waco to meet the Siecks and Meads, we had one option. The only way to Waco was over this bridge.

Waiting for a break in the traffic, we finally rode out onto the bridge, and started across with traffic coming fast behind us. Helen yelled to me, "Ride like you're being chased by a pack of dogs!" With the previous days experience still fresh in our minds, we again sprinted. This time it was cars and trucks chasing us. I'm sure the drivers were impressed by the speed of the two bikers riding with four panniers apiece. We didn't cause a traffic backup, and didn't get even one honking horn from an annoyed driver. We rode onto the shoulder of the highway at the Waco end of the bridge with a whoop and a holler. There were no actual aggressive dogs to chase us, but with all of our previous experience we had no trouble picturing them in our minds. We again felt as if we had won a race.

May 19 was our last full day in Texas. That evening I wrote the following:

There were several aggressive dogs along today's route. Helen has gotten to where her growling at the dogs seems to intimidate them, and they stop in surprise when she gets after them. There was one dog today that deserves special mention. He/she was standing in the driveway of a small Baptist church. As we rode by, this dog walked to the edge of the road with his/her tail wagging, and I swear it looked like he/she was smiling.

This was our last mention of Texas dogs. We both thought the little Baptist dog wanted to apologize for the others. It was like it wanted us to have a good memory of Texas dogs. We appreciated that.

The Race Is On!

Helen's broken elbow a couple of months before we started this bike adventure totally disrupted her conditioning plans. She had to accept the fact she would be getting in condition for the ride while on the road.

Riding over Apache Summit in New Mexico, after dealing with a bad dog, was a good indication she was now in condition to take on anything. It had taken a thousand miles, but she was now fit to ride me into the ground.

Helen is a very competitive person. She surprises me on occasion when she lets me know that we have been competing, and I've lost. Just walking from store to store in a mall can become a race. In retirement, golf had become so competitive I had reduced the number of times I'd play in a week.

The bike adventure had not been a competition as far as I was concerned. We were a team working together to achieve our goal. This all changed in the middle of Texas. While we remained a team, competition crept into the riding.

We both felt like we had accomplished a great deal when we out ran the pack of wild dogs west of Dublin. Two days later, as we rode toward Waco and the long bridge over Lake Waco where we rode "like we were being chased by a pack of dogs," we rode through some hilly country. Up until now, I had always led the way up hills.

About an hour into the day's ride, I was about half way up a hill with Helen following. Suddenly, she passed me with a grin on her face. Nothing needed to be said, I knew at that point she was feeling very fit, and was challenging me to a race. By her accelerating from behind, she was putting distance between us before I figured out what was happening. Accepting her challenge, I accelerated and was slowly reeling her in. Just

126

before the crest of the hill I caught, and then passed her. Her comment was, "I should have waited until I was closer to the top."

From that point on, as we approached a hill, we both started figuring out our strategy and getting in position to win the next race. I will admit I didn't win them all. Perhaps this gives you an idea why my *Travels with Helen* have been memorable experiences.

A Texas rest stop

A Reunion with Old Friends

I have previously mentioned my classmates from Cornell College, Herman Sieck and Bob Mead. They were a couple of small town Iowa boys who became men with me during our college experiences. I played football with Herm and was an

127

usher at his wedding in Tama. Our sophomore year at Cornell, we all joined the Owls' social group, and along with the other Owls, we are all better men because of this friendship.

Herm was posting my daily emails on the Owls' website. Both of them had been following our progress, and emailing me with suggestions for the route. Waco was a place they wanted included. This would be a convenient place to meet for a mini Owls' reunion.

Herm had done some research and arranged for us to stay that night in a motel on highway 6. We found it about a mile past the long bridge over Lake Waco. Shortly after we checked in they both arrived with their wives. I can't tell you how nice it was to actually meet people in the middle of Texas who had been among my best friends for over 40 years.

I had sent several rolls of film to Herm. This was before I had a digital camera, and slides were still the way to make photo memories. Herm had processed the slides, and we had a little slide show in our motel room. We all enjoyed seeing, and talking about the places we had been. Herm and Suzi had a lot of questions. They had looked at the slides, and were wondering what they were seeing.

For lunch we all traveled to Crawford. This is the small town where President George W. Bush has his ranch. We ate at his favorite restaurant. We knew that because it was the only restaurant in town. He wasn't at the ranch that day, so we didn't stop to greet him.

128

Frank with Bob Mead and Herman Sieck

Looking at our maps, I told our friends that it was appropriate for us to have the reunion here to celebrate our being half way home. At that point, we had traveled 1638.3 miles. A month later, when the adventure ended, I determined that we had actually passed the half-way point back in Dublin, but this was close enough for a celebration.

When we all said goodbye that day, we had already made plans to see Herm and Suzi when our route took us almost past where they were living.

The Sieck's had lived for years in Houston, but were now in the process of building a home on Lake Livingston near the town of Coldspring. The plan was for us to meet in the town of Huntsville. They would then drive us to the condo they were renting while the house was being built, and we would stay with them forgoing a motel for the first time in Texas.

Four days later, after riding about 50 miles east from College Station, we noticed a Chevy Suburban pulling off the road ahead of us. A man got out with a camera and took a picture. When he put the camera down, I recognized Herm. He had really gotten interested in this ride and wanted to get an action shot for the Owls' website.

We greeted one another and then rode our bikes on into Huntsville before we put them on the Suburban. We didn't want to load the bikes on the road for fear someone would think we had cheated, and not pedaled all the way.

The stay with Herm and Suzi stretched out to three nights. Our first day with them, we drove into Houston where we got a first class tour, and met their daughter, Debbie. The second day, Herm took us back to Huntsville, and we pedaled the 50 miles to Livingston. They picked us up there. We spent the rest of the day inspecting the new home, and taking a boat ride on the lake.

Early in the morning after our third night, Herm drove us to the point where we had ended the previous day's ride. We unloaded the bikes and started the ride after thanking Herm and Suzi for showing us great Texas hospitality.

Later, Herm told me he had stood by the road praying that we'd be safe as he watched us pedaling down the road. The dogs barking as we rode past their territory let him follow our progress as we rode out of Livingston. When he no longer heard the dogs, he headed back home to wait for my email journal for that day.

We crossed the Sabine River and entered Louisiana the next day. When I asked a local how to pronounce the name of that river he said it was *say-bean*. The stories about Louisiana will have to wait for a bit. I still have a little more to tell about Texas.

Mother's Day

We pedaled south out of Waco before dawn on Mother's Day, Sunday, May 13. I wanted this to be a special day for Helen since she is a special mother. We watched the sun rise on our left as we rode the 32 miles to the town of Marlin, arriving about 8:00. Our plan was to stop here, get a motel room to change into something more appropriate for church, and celebrate Mother's Day worshiping with brothers and sisters in Christ.

As had happened before, we arrived before the only motel in town had cleaned their rooms. People might have still been in bed for that matter. We were told to wait for an hour or two

131

and they would have something for us. With no options, we took advantage of the time to ride around Marlin looking for a church with a sign listing the time of services. There was a large Baptist church in the center of town with a service starting at 11:00. We would be worshipping with the Baptists for Mother's Day.

After breakfast at Los Pepes (the only restaurant we found), we checked into the Relax Inn. By 11:00 we were back at the First Baptist Church of Marlin. I had noticed that while churches all have parking lots for cars, they usually don't have a bike rack. We locked our bikes together in front of the church under the gaze of a lot of Baptists who had to be wondering who these people were arriving at church on bicycles. Finally breaking the ice and asking, they were amazed when we told them we had come from San Diego, and were heading home to Florida.

The question that often followed where we were going was to ask why we were doing this on bikes. It is not easy to explain to people unless they also have a sense of adventure. They didn't believe me when I said it was because we couldn't afford gas for a car. The Baptists in Marlin were genuinely pleased we had stopped. We caused quite a stir among the congregation that only ended when the worship service started.

The pastor honored all the mothers, and then announced he had a gift for a special mother who had traveled the greatest distance for the service that day. Everyone in the service looked, and pointed to Helen. She won this contest *hands down*. The gift was the book *The Prayer of Jabez* that was popular in

2001. Helen was honored to receive this recognition. The down side was she also had one more item to carry back to Florida in her panniers.

Both Mike and Brad had sent email Mother's Day greetings. Mike urged me to take Helen to a nice restaurant. Los Pepes was as nice as there was in Marlin. The only other place to eat was the Dairy Queen. After church, we celebrated the day with a DQ blizzard before heading back to the Relax Inn to prepare for the next day's ride.

A President and Horses

The day after Mother's Day, we continued to ride south. The town of Calvert had a sign announcing that it was the *antique capital of Texas*. There have been a lot of antique shops along our route, so the *antique capital* must be something to see.

In my email that evening I wrote the following:

In Calvert, we met a man named Roy. Roy was amazed at what we were doing. He sat down on a bench with Helen and told us about his experiences as a driver for some wealthy Houston banker and an oilman named Bush. I think Roy would have liked it if we had stayed talking with him all morning, but we had miles to ride before the wind came up. We told him goodbye, and he told us to stay safe. I think I would have understood more Roy had to say if he had put in his teeth this morning.

Sixty-five miles from Marlin we arrived in College Station. We had thought about stopping earlier, but when we committed to riding past our first goal, we got caught up in traffic approaching Bryan. Taking a by-pass we ended up just south of Bryan in College Station, the home of Texas A & M University. A sign directing traffic to the George Bush Presidential Library got our attention, and the decision was made that College Station was our home for the night. The Super 8 motel was near the University which made it easy for us to tour the campus, and check out the Presidential Library the next day.

Helen found the wildflowers along the road in Texas were a good spot to rest and cool off her feet.

This Presidential Library was for President George H. W. Bush. His son had taken office just a couple months before we departed on this cross-continent adventure. If all presidential libraries are as interesting as this, I'd encourage you to make a point to stop if you are ever near one. It had displays starting from his childhood as well as historic items, and documents from his government service. A sculpture of horses leaping over a fallen Berlin Wall stands outside in front of the library. Looking at it brought back memories of when the wall was literally torn down by German youths to free the people of East Berlin from the imprisonment of Communism. I have a chunk of that wall that was given to me by, Mary Sloan, a teacher at Page Traditional School where I worked. Her son was in college doing a semester abroad when this historic event took place. He brought home several chunks of the wall, and I was honored to get one of them.

As Helen and I looked at this work of art, we commented on how familiar the horses looked. As we had ridden out of Ruidoso, New Mexico, we passed the Ruidoso Downs quarter horse race track. I had stopped to take a photo of a sculpture of running horses that is in front of the track. We asked about the artist who did the work at the library, and learned it was the same person. If you are ever near College Station, this sculpture is worth driving out of your way to see. Here is the photo.

135

Leaving Texas

Like the horses in the photo, Helen and I were about to "break out" of Texas. May 20, a week after Mother's Day, found us crossing the border to Louisiana. The East Texas countryside with Spanish moss on the oak trees was beginning to look like country with which we could identify. However, we had some trouble finding the border.

The last real town we rode through in Texas was Newton. Riding east out of town, Helen expressed concern we had somehow gotten on the wrong road. I reminded her that I'm the one on this team with an internal compass. I was certain we were on the correct road. After a mile or so, and not having seen markers for highway 190, I started to have my doubts. As hard as it was, I confessed to Helen I was no longer certain we were on highway 190.

I have often explained to Helen that just because I don't know where I am doesn't mean I'm lost. Even after all these years traveling with me, Helen has not bought into this concept. Of course, she wanted to stop and get directions. That is something I hate to do. She pointed out that if we had a car, driving around to find the road would be one thing, but getting around with leg power was a waste of energy. In spite of my objections, Helen stopped at a little country church, and asked if we were on highway 190? She was thrilled to get the word that we had missed a turn in the middle of town. I was eating humble pie for the rest of that day.

The Sabine River was significant not only as the border between Texas and Louisiana. It was the border between the

United States and New Spain after the Louisiana Purchase in 1803. I'm writing this on September 16, 2011. Two hundred years ago today Mexico declared independence from Spain. After a long War for Independence, the Sabine River became the border between the United States and the independent country of Mexico.

The young country of Mexico had difficulty controlling this border. Americans flocked illegally to Texas in such numbers they soon became a problem for the Mexican government. (Does this sound familiar today in reverse?) The Battle of the Alamo in San Antonio was a result of these problems. That battle was followed by the Battle of San Jacinto near Houston where Texas gained their independence.

When Texas became a part of the United States, there was a question as to the location of the border. The Mexicans claimed it was the Nueces River that flows into the Gulf of Mexico at Corpus Christi. The Texans and the United States, said it was the Rio Grande. This border question was resolved by the war with Mexico in the 1840's. That war not only established the border as the Rio Grande, but made all the land we had covered from San Diego to the Sabine River officially United States territory.

As we pedaled across the Sabine River, I had no idea how many times in the next ten years my *Travels with Helen* would take me across the Rio Grande into Mexico. The adventure we were on in May of 2001 was preparing us for other adventures to follow, but I'm getting ahead of my story. See you in Louisiana in the next chapter.

137

CHAPTER 6

Louisiana
May 20 to May 28, 2001

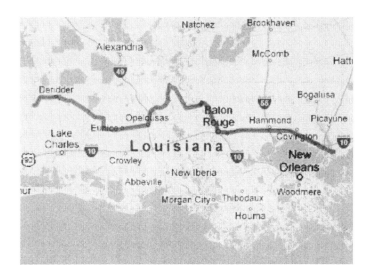

Cajun Country

After crossing the Sabine River into Louisiana, we rode for another 30 miles to the town of DeRidder. In my email journal for May 20 I wrote, *Helen gives the roads in Louisiana an A as she is sitting in the Red Carpet Inn eating the last of Suzi Sieck's chocolate chip cookies."* In just two days, that grade would plummet, but the cookies retained a grade of A.

I was looking forward to being in Cajun country and learning something about the culture I'd heard so much about. We were told we weren't yet in Cajun country, but we would be there after traveling a little further east.

The Cajuns were originally called Arcadians. They were Frenchmen who settled in what was known as Arcadia in eastern Canada and Maine. During the French and Indian War in the 1750's, they were expelled from the British colonies. Many of them traveled to New Orleans and settled in the area in Louisiana west of the Mississippi River. Somehow the name changed from Arcadian to Cajun.

The lighted clock on the Beauregard Parrish Courthouse (the name for counties in Louisiana) was at 4:55 a.m. when we rode out of DeRidder to get an early start ahead of the predicted thunderstorms and wind.

When we stopped at the White Sands Canoe Rental, after riding about thirty miles, I again asked if we were in Cajun country. The person said this wasn't Cajun country, but we would be in Cajun country when we got to Oberlin. Oberlin was only ten miles further down the road. Evidently, there is a definite border that isn't observable to the unaware traveler.

Oberlin was indeed a Cajun town. After checking in at the Oberlin Motel, we walked across to the Depot Café for breakfast. Having just sat down, we were startled by a train whistle. A Union Pacific train was rolling past right next to the café and about half a block from our motel. The people in the café noticed our surprise, and said you get used to the whistle. It didn't bother them. They also said the trains passed through all day and night. This left us wondering if we were going to get any sleep that night.

I found a barber shop after breakfast. Stanton Reed was a proud Cajun about my age who was eager to share stories about growing up, and living all his life in this culture. Before he could enter first grade in the Oberlin School, he had to learn English. Up until then he had only known French. His grandmother never did learn English.

All the time Stanton was talking and telling stories, he was cutting my hair. No other customers had come in, so he was in no hurry for me to leave. My hair was getting shorter and shorter. Helen finally came looking for me just before I was sure Stanton was going to finish off the last of my hair with a razor. Helen's expression said I may not need another hair cut before Christmas.

At the restaurant where we ate that evening, our waitress was a high school student. Since we were the only customers, she shared some interesting observations with us. It was her feeling that her generation was losing a lot of the French culture. She wasn't happy about it. The only foreign language in her school is Spanish. Her grandparents only speak French. It would have made sense to her to have French as the language elective.

We asked about the mural we had seen on a side of a building. She told us the building needed a coat of paint at the time a muralist came through town. He offered to paint a mural depicting the history and culture of Oberlin. The building owner and the town shared the cost. As we studied the mural on our way back to the motel, we got a better feel for the Cajun culture. We also slept through the train whistles.

The Oberlin mural

Since Oberlin, we have observed many murals in towns all across our land. It is worth the time to stop and study them. You are bound to learn something about the town and its culture.

Our ride the next day from Oberlin to Opelousas was all in Cajun country. The day started well, but about half way to

Opelousas it deteriorated big time. At one point we had to ride through a construction site and a big truck actually forced me off the road. I didn't fall, but it was scary to be riding down into a deep ditch.

That evening, I wrote the following; *Louisiana is the fifth state in which Helen and I have ridden on our cross-country bicycle adventure. We decided today that Louisiana ranks fifth in all categories except ugly dogs. The roads are poor, the drivers cut us off and crowd us off the road, people can't give good directions, and the food is spicy.*

Louisiana was full of emotional highs and lows. Oberlin had been a good experience and our favorite town on the whole trip was not far ahead. In the end, however, we were happy to escape from Louisiana a step ahead of the police. Before I tell you about this adventure, we have to find a way to cross the Mississippi River.

Crossing the Mississippi River

Opelousas is the third oldest city in Louisiana having been founded in 1720. Helen's comment was that after almost 300 years it was about time they repaved the streets.

Jim Bowie of knife and Alamo fame was one of many famous people who had lived in Opelousas. I was disappointed that the only Bowie Knife in the Hall of Fame Museum was a replica and not the real thing. Like all museums, this one was interesting, and worth the time we took to go through it.

I decided I couldn't leave the Cajun country without trying to eat some crawdads. Getting directions to an authentic Cajun restaurant from people in Opelousas was a challenge. Our first set of instructions took us north all the way out of town. I sometimes think people don't want to admit they don't know where something is, so they just make it up figuring that by the time you learn they had given bogus directions you wouldn't be able to find them to complain.

When we finally found a restaurant featuring Cajun crawdads, they were served in a plastic basket lined with red and white paper. Plastic forks were the utensils. Actually, I liked the crawdads, which made me think I could have had a lot of meals growing up in Early, Iowa; if I'd known then you could eat the crawdads we boys liked to catch in Digger's Creek.

To the east of Opelousas is Mississippi River delta country. There appeared to be only two east-west roads in this part of Louisiana. Between where we were and the Mississippi River is the Atchafalaya Basin. We needed to cross a lot of small and a couple large, world class rivers to get east of the Mississippi. The map indicated three bridges across the Atchafalaya. One of them is the very long Interstate 10 Bridge to our south, and a definite no-no road for bicycles. Directly in front of us is another miles long no-no bridge on highway 190. We investigated this road riding east for a couple of miles before coming to signs warning about this route. The other possibility was going north to Simmesport where we could cross the Atchafalaya and then ride south along the Mississippi to a ferry.

144

Check out the haircut.

This last option was the one recommended on our Southern Tier Route map. The discouraging thing about this route was that Simmesport was 50 miles almost due north of Opelousas. I thought it would be nice to go more easterly.

There was another road on the map that looked promising, but I needed more information before taking it. This mysterious road was just a little line on the state road map. It wasn't even mentioned on my route map.

About nine miles north of Opelousas, we stopped early in the morning at a little coffee shop in the small town of Washington. There were several men sitting at tables drinking their coffee and talking. I walked over, and asked if they might help us. I mentioned how we were looking for a more direct road to St. Francisville. They all pointed to one man, and told me he was the one who had built most of the roads in this area. I didn't want to upset him, so I didn't comment on what we thought of his roads.

I showed him my Louisiana road map, and pointed out the mysterious road with the bridge. After studying the map, he told me this was really a ferry, and the road on the other side was gravel. There was some discussion among the coffee shop men about whether or not this ferry was still running. It didn't sound very promising. Our *advisor* said the route we were on to Simmesport was our best bet. We thanked him, and got back on the bikes riding north.

Twenty miles later, we came to Lebeau. Inquiring about the ferry that was nearby, I was told it had been shutdown. Evidently it was used so little that no one in Washington had noticed its disappearance.

As we continued our ride north to Simmesport, I mentioned to Helen how the soil looked a lot like what I remembered in Iowa. Then it occurred to me that at one time this soil might have been in Iowa. It had all come down the Missouri and Mississippi Rivers to end up in Louisiana.

The cemeteries we rode by that day caught our attention. The graves all seemed to be above or partly above the ground. Digging a hole that wouldn't fill with water is probably a challenge here in the delta. Once we get across the Mississippi I'll share something I learned about these graves.

Louisiana graveyard

The Sportsmen's Motel in Simmesport had the distinction of being the closest in quality to the motel in Salome, Arizona. If we hadn't stopped in Salome, the Sportsmen's Motel would have been at the bottom of the rating scale.

The next morning we crossed a long, high bridge over the Atchafalaya River just south of where it branches off from the Mississippi River. The rest of the morning we rode mostly south along the Mississippi River. All we saw was the bank of a very high levee. I felt I was riding next to a high wall. It has taken a lot of engineering skill and lots of high levees to keep the rivers here where the government wants them.

While riding in Texas, I had picked up a *USA Today* newspaper, and looking through it found an article in the travel section about the big trees in Louisiana. The location of these trees was on the road we were taking south from Simmesport. St. Francisville, our next stop was mentioned prominently in the

147

article. We were watching for the trees, and were not disappointed. These trees were ancient. The article stated they were as large in circumference as some of the giant redwoods in California.

One of the big trees

Forty miles from Simmesport, we rode up to the top of the levee, and had our first good look at the mighty Mississippi River. It was an awesome sight. The river water was flowing past the ferry landing with a force that almost took away my breath. My first reaction was "this is one mighty river." All the water from the Ohio River, the Missouri River and everything in between was flowing at our feet. This powerful river made me and my bike seem awfully insignificant.

Soon after we stopped and were inspired by the mighty river, cars started to arrive and line up for boarding the ferry. In

148

about fifteen minutes, I saw the boat churning its way towards us through the fast moving current.

Helen and I got more for our money on the ferry ride than the people in the automobiles. While we stood at the rail hearing the roar of the water pushing against the ferry boat trying to wash us all downstream to the Gulf of Mexico, everyone else sat in their car with the A/C on listening to their music.

At 2140 miles we crossed the Mississippi River on a ferry

We had reached another milestone when we crossed this great river. It was like we had now left the west behind and were heading into the home stretch. On the east side of the river, we waited while all the cars drove off the ferry and then up the bluff that was in front of us.

Just downstream from the ferry landing was a paddle wheel river boat. Tourists were walking off this boat, and heading to the buses that would drive them into the town of St. Francisville. Some of these tourists thought we were one of the tourist attractions. They took our pictures, and seemed to want to interview us. In return, we questioned them. I hadn't realized there are paddle wheel cruise boats taking tourists up and down the Mississippi River.

After the tourist buses drove their passengers down the road to St. Francisville, Helen and I pedaled along behind the diesel fumes, and soon rode into what we now consider our favorite town on this long, adventurous journey.

This is the photo the tourists wanted for their photo album.

St. Francisville, Louisiana

St. Francisville is situated on hills on the east side of the Mississippi River. West of the great river, the land was very flat. Before the levee system was constructed, annual floods were expected in these low lands. The flood water was so strong it often washed bodies out of graves. In the late 1700's, someone got the idea of having the cemetery on the higher ground on the east side of the river. Once they had the cemetery, people realized this was a good place to live, and thus was founded the town of St. Francisville.

The Louisiana Purchase brought all of Louisiana west of the Mississippi River into the United States. The east side, including the gulf coast counties of Mississippi and Alabama, remained a possession of Spain, and was called Spanish West Florida. This is a part of our country's history often not included in school history classes. You might want to do some independent study to learn more about how this land became part of the United States.

An interesting bit of St. Francisville history took place in June of 1863. At this time in the Civil War, the Union was trying to gain control of the Mississippi River. General Grant had laid siege to Vicksburg, Mississippi, which is north of St. Francisville. The confederates controlled well fortified Fort Hudson between St. Francisville and Baton Rouge. The river between Fort Hudson, south of St. Francisville, and Vicksburg was what was being contested.

Only two Union gunboats made it past Fort Hudson, and were on their way to support the siege of Vicksburg. The commander of one of gunboats, the USS Albatross, died, as they passed St. Francisville. His dying request was to have a Masonic funeral. No one onboard the gunboat could conduct this service. A small party with a flag of truce went ashore at St.

Francisville to see if a Masonic burial could be arranged. The Masons in St. Francisville agreed to conduct the service.

The next day the funeral service was conducted by a Confederate officer. A one day truce was declared for all the troops in the area of St. Francisville. This event is celebrated each year in St. Francisville as *The Day the War Stopped.* We saw signs advertising this annual celebration to take place in a week.

St. Francisville was shelled by Union gunboats several times during the war. I like to think the USS Albatross wasn't one of them.

Helen and I stayed at the St. Francisville Inn. This Bed and Breakfast inn is surrounded by Spanish moss covered oaks and magnolia trees. It is on the edge of the restored antebellum section of this historic town. The restoration reminded us a little of Colonial Williamsburg. We had time after checking in at the inn to walk through this area and visit the museum. We even found the cemetery at Grace Episcopal Church where the commander of the Albatross was buried.

Our last rest day had been at Lake Livingston in Texas when we stayed with Herm and Suzi Sieck. After going over the 2000 mile mark and crossing the Mississippi River, we had earned another day off.

The St. Francisville Inn

Laurie and Pat were our hosts at the inn, and made us feel very welcome. We got what we thought was good advice regarding routes going east. They also told us some St. Francisville stories. As we sat around the breakfast table talking with them we were joined by Valerie and Richard McFarlane. They entered into the story telling also. After a bit, Valerie and Richard asked us what our plans were for the day. We replied that we were going to be riding our bikes around the area to visit a couple of the antebellum plantation homes. They had the same plans, so invited us to ride with them in their rental car. It took us less than a second to accept this kind invitation.

Valerie and Richard talked a little differently, and we soon found out why. They are from England, and now live in Hong Kong. They were on holiday touring the United States. We had a delightful time with them.

153

Our first stop was Oakley Plantation. This West Indies style home was built about 1806. The most famous person to live in St. Francisville was John James Audubon. The owner of Oakley Plantation hired Audubon in 1821 to tutor his teen-aged daughter. After three months, Audubon was *let go*. I don't know why he was laid off, but during his time at Oakley Plantation he did 32 of his famous bird paintings. He shot the birds, and then made the paintings from their dead carcasses. The average painting took 3 days, which was probably as long as he could stand to have the dead bird sitting on his desk. Touring the inside of the house, we saw his room and the equipment he used to get the birds and make the paintings.

From Oakley we went to Rosedown Plantation. Here we visited not only the Greek revival style home, but the large beautiful formal gardens. The drive up to the front of this home was definitely a "Kodak moment."

When the plantations around St. Francisville were working farms and not tourist attractions, they produced huge crops of sugar. Some plantations had their own landings on the Mississippi River for getting the crop to New Orleans and beyond. Of course, the labor on the plantations was all done by slaves. Their quarters didn't look like the homes we photographed.

At Oakley Plantation

As Helen and I prepared to pedal away from St. Francisville we made a promise to one another that at some time in the not too distant future we would return, and visit other plantations,

155

and these friendly people. Home was still a thousand miles to our east.

Rosedown Plantation

Our Escape from Louisiana

At St. Francisville, we left our planned route through the southern tier of states. Our camping gear had only been used three times in the West. Surely we didn't need to continue lugging it the rest of the way to Florida. I was certain that east of Texas we would not be in any places without motels. Herm and Suzi Sieck shipped the tent and sleeping bags to Melbourne Beach after we left their home at Lake Livingston. Now in St. Francisville, where we had crossed the Mississippi River, we had a problem. The planned route east into the state of Mississippi looked like we would need to camp. I'd made a miscalculation. The solution was to find a route where we knew there would be motels, and this required our making a detour

156

heading south rather than east from St. Francisville. Going south would take us to Baton Rouge, and from there we would turn east and south to the Gulf Coast and plenty of motels.

In preparation for our long ride, I had read that adventure starts when your trip plans take a detour. Finding our way out of Louisiana involved some big *detours* resulting in several additional adventures.

Going south from St. Francisville seemed to be working until we were leaving Baton Rouge on highway 190 heading east. This was definitely not a biker friendly road. There was no shoulder. The traffic was very heavy, and the drivers seemed to be very annoyed that two people on bicycles were trying to share their space. In desperation, we found a side road that took us to an interchange with Interstate 12 where we could find a motel, and figure out where we were going next. In riding past the ramp leading up to the interstate highway, I noticed there was no sign prohibiting bicycles on the road. Most interstate highways have signs prohibiting bicycles and pedestrians. We had found in the West, however, many times bikes were permitted to use the interstate if it was the only route between two points. We decided Louisiana was like Arizona and would not mind our using Interstate 12.

Before dawn the next day we were on the interstate and making good progress when I noticed flashing lights coming up behind me. The Louisiana State trooper who pulled us over pointed out we were not allowed on the interstate highway. When I mentioned there were no signs, he explained that the state is poor, and can't afford them. We declined his offer to give us a lift to the next exit, and explained our problems with traffic the day before. The trooper agreed that the broad shoulders of Interstate 12 were a safer place than with the traffic on highway 190. He even told us he would call headquarters, and let them know we had his permission to be riding on Interstate 12. "No one will be bothering you the rest of the way," he said. With his blessing we continued on the interstate highway, and had a great ride until we ran into a big, disastrous detour.

The morning was a pleasant ride on our personal bike trail next to Interstate 12. After about 50 miles, with Helen following close behind, I swerved to the left to avoid a piece of glass. At that instant, Helen's front wheel overlapped my rear wheel. My swerve made our wheels touch. I didn't feel a thing, but heard a noise behind me. Looking back, I saw Helen lying on the ground by her bike. Dropping mine, I ran back to her. She wasn't moving, and when I knelt down by her motionless body I realized she was unconscious.

I had no idea what to do. I couldn't get any response from Helen. I've seen people pass out, but never stay out for so long. Here we were next to an interstate highway with only our bikes for transportation. I tried to think of a way I could get her on my bike, and take her to a hospital. Obviously I wasn't thinking very clearly.

Praying, "Lord I don't know what to do. Please bring someone to help Helen." As I opened my eyes, it was with a great sense of comfort that I saw the Lord was already answering my prayer. First a car and then a pick-up pulled onto the shoulder in front of us. Several people ran over to lend a hand. As they rushed to our sides, I was astonished to see an ambulance stopping. About this time, Helen started to regain consciousness asking questions like, "Are we in Florida?" and "What are all these people doing in my bedroom?"

The EMTs bandaged Helen's leg and arm, and checked out her head. The medics wanted to take her to a hospital, but since she seemed to be coming around I talked them out of it. They gave me instructions as to what symptoms I should be looking for in case Helen had a concussion problem during the rest of the day and night. Danny and his son in the pick-up offered to give us a ride to the next town, Covington.

While the ambulance crew was working on Helen, a state trooper drove through the interstate highway median with lights flashing and pulled up behind us. I thought he was coming to see if he could be of assistance. His first comments put that thought out of my mind. All he was interested in was punishing us for daring to ride our bikes on his interstate highway. I explained we had been given permission earlier, but he would hear none of that. Helen argued with him as well, which indicated she was feeling herself again. (To this day, Helen has no memory of the confrontation with this police officer.) I let the trooper know we were through riding for the day, and that Danny was giving us a lift to Covington. His reply was for me to wait while he wrote up my ticket because, "I was in big trouble with the State of Louisiana." I'm sure I had some smart comment to make as he walked back to his patrol car. I turned my back on him, and went back to helping with Helen.

159

After a few minutes, I looked around for the trooper, and my ticket. To my surprise, his patrol car was gone. I mentioned to one of the EMTs I had been told to wait for my ticket. She said the officer had told her he called his commander at headquarters to find out the number of the law I'd broken. They couldn't find it, so he couldn't site our violation on the ticket. Perhaps someone at headquarters had told him we had permission, and he wasn't to give us any trouble. For whatever reason, we didn't get a ticket. Helen's sore body was enough punishment.

I put our bikes and all our gear in Danny's pick-up. Before we got in with Danny for the ride to Covington, I thanked everyone for their help. I was curious how the ambulance had gotten to us so fast. I didn't think ambulances cruised around looking for customers like taxis. The EMTs said there had not been a call for us. They were responding to a call for an accident a couple of miles farther down the road. The strange thing, they said, was that just before they saw us they were notified there wasn't an accident, and they should come back to their station. They saw us right after they were called off the original call, and decided to stop to see if we needed any help. The impression we got was that it was very unusual for an ambulance to be called off an accident call. We thanked the Lord for that call. He had sent the ambulance on its way before Helen had fallen!

Danny and his son dropped us off at a Best Western Motel in Covington. As we checked-in, we noticed on the motel meeting announcement board that a church was having a service

160

in a meeting room in about an hour. We cleaned up as much as we could, and headed for the church service.

The pastor, Bill Lee, greeted us. We enjoyed talking with him, and telling how we happened to be in Covington. After a while, we noticed that no one else had come for the service. It was only Helen, Bill and me. He explained this was a brand new church, and so far very few people were attending. Since this was Memorial Day weekend, he knew that all of the regular attendees would be out of town. He felt he should come anyway, and had prepared a sermon even though he hadn't expected anyone to be there. Helen and I sat in chairs while Bill stood behind his lectern and gave us his whole sermon. It was obvious it was meant just for us.

That day the Lord had not only put us in a position where there was no way we could solve problems ourselves, but He had sent people all day to look out for us. The detour that seemed like a disaster was the Lord teaching us to depend on Him. As He said in Joshua 1:9 *He is with us always*. By making our trip an adventure, God was using it to put us in His will.

Helen did not suffer any ill-effects from her fall and the next morning, before sunrise, we were back on Interstate 12 riding east to Mississippi for what we called *our escape from Louisiana*. That was our last interstate highway travel on the bicycles, but not the end of our adventure.

CHAPTER 7

MISSISSIPPI
May 28 to May 30

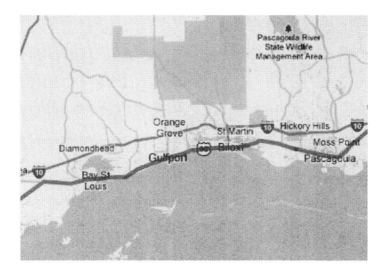

We exited Interstate Highway 12 at Slidell, Louisiana, and coasted into a Shell station at the end of the exit ramp congratulating each other for having ridden 20 miles on the interstate without a single run-in with a Louisiana State Trooper.

Helen was proving to be a real *Road Warrior*. I tried to talk her into taking a rest day in Covington to make sure she had no after-effects from her bad fall the day before. She insisted that we get out early and make our escape before the cops could find us. I had to admire her. She was like a football player who plays hurt. Thank the Lord; she had no lingering problems from her BIG fall.

We got good directions for how to get to Mississippi in the Slidell Shell station. Everyone there getting gas or a cup of coffee had advice, but one fellow seemed to be more confident in his directions, and they proved to be perfect. The problem with Slidell is that three interstate highways converge, and traffic is funneled south to New Orleans. Getting past these highways and to highway 90 was our problem. Following the directions, we maneuvered through residential sections of the town, and after what seemed like negotiating a maze we found ourselves at the east edge of Slidell on highway 90.

A few miles east we crossed the Pearl River and entered the state of Mississippi. With each state we entered, we became more eager to get home. The countryside was looking more and more like Florida. The live oaks with the Spanish moss and the magnolias with the beautiful white blossoms, gave it a homey appearance. We also knew we were close to gulf coast beaches, and these were definitely drawing us home.

164

We stayed in Waveland our first of two nights in Mississippi. The next day we were on the road early. Traffic was light as we pedaled east out of Waveland, and passed through the town of Bay St. Louis. The high bridge over St. Louis Bay gave us our first look at the Gulf of Mexico off to our right. As we pedaled through the next town, Pass Christian, traffic started building, and by the time we reached Gulfport the traffic was like what we had encountered near Baton Rouge a few days earlier.

Highway 90 is a four lane road passing right beside the beach. As we pedaled along we had miles of beautiful sand beaches on our right. However, the cars whizzing past kept us from enjoying the view. At places we could ride on a boardwalk, but these only lasted for a block or two before we were funneled back onto the highway. We tried to ride as close to the right side of the road as possible in order to avoid the traffic. This was as stressful a morning ride as we had on the whole cross-continent adventure.

The night before, in Waveland, I had inspected Helen's helmet. From her fall the day before on the interstate highway, there were three cracks running from the bottom all the way to the top. It took a lot of force to break that helmet. No wonder Helen had been unconscious. We knew this helmet had saved her life. Now we needed to replace it.

Using the yellow pages in the motel room, we looked for bike shops where we could find Helen's replacement helmet. The Wheel House in a strip mall on highway 90 in Biloxi was the closest bike shop we could find near our route.

165

We located the Wheel House after battling our way through the Gulfport traffic. The sign on the door indicated it wouldn't be open for business for another hour and a half. We killed time by going to the nearby Waffle House for breakfast, and then sitting on the beach.

Richard finally came and opened the Wheel House. We were his first customers for the day. Helen picked out her replacement helmet, and the cracked one that had saved her life was laid to rest in Richard's trashcan.

After we made the purchase, Richard asked questions about our ride. I had the feeling he would like to have this adventure in the future. I mentioned the problems with riding in the traffic on highway 90, and asked if there was another route we could use through Biloxi. He told me that 90 was really the best route. The advice he gave was to ride in the middle of the right lane rather than at the right curb

"Ride in such a way that cars won't try to squeeze past you. Out in the lane, they'll have to pass just like you were a slow moving car," was his advice. He reminded us we had as much right to the road as the cars. While we knew that, we had to wonder if the drivers would see it that way.

Back on the road, Richard's suggestion worked very well. Generally, we were able to keep up with the traffic. No one was beeping their horn or making unfriendly gestures as they passed. The rest of the ride was much less stressful, and happily, Helen never gave her new helmet a serious test.

Our plan for this day was to get as far as Pascagoula. We were sure to find a nice place there to spend our second night in

Mississippi. It would also be our last night in Mississippi. Alabama would be close, but we weren't going to cross the border today since we weren't sure we could find anywhere to stay near the border on the Alabama side.

Our last hurdle before the town of Pascagoula was a long bridge over the Pascagoula River. As we rode up to the west end of this bridge, my mind went back to the long bridge over Lake Waco back in Texas. There didn't seem to be a shoulder on this bridge either. On top of that, there was construction. As we studied the situation, Helen pointed out that it looked like the construction on the left lanes of the bridge was completed, and the orange barrels were there just to protect the workers as they were cleaning up. That looked like a good bike trail, so we headed for the left side of the bridge. After riding about a quarter mile, we got to the construction workers. I asked if they would mind our riding on the part that seemed to be finished but not yet open for cars. They told us to go ahead, and seemed to have no problems with our winding our way through their work. We felt special, like we had our own private highway as we cruised past the cars that were creeping along bumper to bumper.

Our special feeling ended, however, when we got to the end of the construction. In our front was a draw bridge over the river channel. We had no option but to get back on the road with the cars we had passed on the way over. When there was a break in traffic, we darted out and then came to a screeching halt. We had not noticed the draw bridge being raised. That's why there was a break in traffic. We had ridden so far up the

167

side of the bridge that the gate came down behind us as the bridge came up in front of us. We stood by the raised span as a shrimp boat passed under. Dashing across ahead of the cars when the bridge was lowered made us feel like we were pretty hot stuff.

Our search for home that night in Pascagoula did not go well. Every motel we found reminded us too much of Salome, Arizona, or Simmesport, Louisiana. At the east side of town, we had run out of motels. What were we going to do? Camping wasn't an option since our camping gear had already made it back to Florida from Texas. Then I remembered the interstate highway was several miles to our north. If we could find a road going north to an interchange, we should be able to find a motel for the night.

Interstate highways have become like the railroads in the 1800's. Little towns were established every few miles along the railroad right of way to provide services to the farmers living in the area. Now the interchanges along the interstate highways have lodging, food, and fuel services for travelers. Finding interchange 69 on Interstate Highway 10 was the solution to our dilemma. Our day ended at the Days Inn in Moss Point, Mississippi. This was 61 miles from Waveland and 2336 miles from our beginning in San Diego. We considered these 61 miles as somewhat courageous. Riding in the middle of the right lane in heavy traffic, and creating our own bridge was not for the faint of heart.

168

Waiting for the bridge to close

CHAPTER 8

ALABAMA
May 30 to June 1, 2001

It is obvious in the photograph we entered Alabama early in the morning. Helen liked getting started before it was light. I went along with her, but didn't like it. When we get to the Florida chapter, I'll have more to say about these early starts.

The issue in riding through the Gulf Coast of Alabama was getting around Mobile Bay. The Adventure Cycling Southern Tier Route had two ways to get past Mobile Bay. One option was to go south along the west shore of the bay to Dauphin Island and then cross the mouth of the bay by ferry. The other option was to go through the city of Mobile and then south on the east shore to Gulf Shores. When we made the decision in St. Francisville, Louisiana, to go south to Baton Rouge, we were also committing ourselves to the Dauphin Island option.

We rejoined the Southern Tier Route at Grand Bay, Alabama. I had to wonder how our ride would have been different if we had followed the map to this point instead of forging our own route that included the Interstate 12 adventure. I'll never know about that route. We were not about to turn around and start over.

The day's ride to Dauphin Island was one of our most pleasant days of riding. The roads were good and traffic was light. We needed a day like this after the Mississippi Gulf Coast.

The final leg of the ride to Dauphin Island was on a five mile bridge with a wide shoulder. This island is a barrier island like the one where we live in Florida. The sand dunes and beach looked much like Melbourne Beach. One difference was the oil platforms we could see just off the coast.

Dauphin Island was first settled by the French in 1699. Later it was controlled by the Spanish and the British. Whoever controlled Dauphin Island controlled access to Mobile Bay which made it a very strategic location. In 1813, the island was captured by the Americans. This forced the Spanish to give up its West Florida Territory, and all the country we had pedaled through since St. Francisville then became a part of the United States.

During the Civil War, the control of Mobile Bay was essential for the Confederacy. They needed the port at Mobile to receive supplies from European countries. To keep the bay in their control, two large forts were built. Fort Gaines was on Dauphin Island and Fort Morgan was on the east side of the mouth of the bay. The Battle of Mobile Bay took place in these waters in August of 1864. It was during this battle that Admiral Farragut gave the famous order, "Damn the torpedoes, full speed ahead."

The next morning we boarded a ferry for the ride from Fort Gaines to Fort Morgan across the mouth of Mobile Bay. We enjoyed starting our day with a boat ride. The boat had to weave its way through the oil platforms as we cruised east.

Besides weaving around oil platforms, we had another surprising experience that day. When we got to the town of Gulf Shores we found a designated bike lane on the side of the highway. The last time I remember a bike lane was way back in Phoenix. As we pedaled along the beach on the bike lane, Helen's comment was, "this is heavenly."

173

This was on a Thursday. The next city we would pedal through was Pensacola, Florida, and it was just a few miles ahead. After our experience with rush hour traffic back in Mississippi, we had decided to enjoy the nice gulf beach and wait for Saturday to take on Pensacola.

The Mobile Bay ferry

We checked in at a Days Inn in Orange Beach that was right on the gulf. Since we were planning to stay for two nights I inquired about the second night, and was told the room rate would be doubled for that night. I was shocked. The clerk said their tourist season starts on June 1, and that was tomorrow. Doing some research before committing to the second night, I discovered that in Florida the season was different. By riding nine miles the next morning, we could get a room in Perdido Key, Florida, much cheaper than in Orange Beach, Alabama. We took the beach room for one night.

174

The next morning, after the complimentary breakfast and coffee on the beach, we packed and headed for Florida. Just as we arrived at the state line, the heavens opened and we were hit with a deluge. Riding on was not possible. We could see Florida right in front of us; could almost touch it in fact. The road flooded as we made haste to the awning over the door of a Waffle House.

Alabama had been a nice two day bike ride. However, we were feeling trapped as we tried to make our way out.

Whenever we stopped at a Waffle House, I'd have one waffle and Helen would have two. Don't know how she can eat twice as many waffles as I can, but she does. We decided this was an early lunch and not a second breakfast as we waited for the downpour to stop.

Finally, we were able to get back on the road for our shortest day's ride on this cross-continent adventure; nine miles from Orange Beach, Alabama, to Perdido Key, Florida. In my daily email journal, I referred to the short ride as a relocation/rest day. We were now on the homestretch.

CHAPTER 9

FLORIDA
June 1 to June 15, 2001

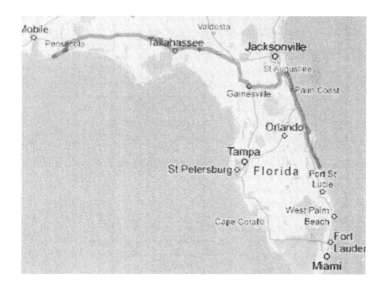

The Florida Panhandle

The rain that had us pinned down on the Alabama side of the border finally let up and we were able to enter Florida. In the photo above you can see the water puddles in the sand as we were leaving the Waffle House.

The nine miles to the Perdido Key Best Western Motel was just enough to get the waffles settled. For all practical purposes this was a rest day. I took advantage of the time off to do some routine bike maintenance and cleaning. The bike supplies were an added weight that I didn't want to carry along, so on rest days I sought out bike shops where I could buy some lubricant and chain cleaning fluid. There was a bike shop within easy walking distance on Perdido Key and the walk helped get the waffles settled even more.

Our plan to avoid traffic in Pensacola worked perfectly. We had a nice ride along the waterfront of this old city, and then rode north along Escambia Bay before we turned east again on highway 90. This highway took us almost all the way across the Florida Panhandle.

I suspect it is human nature to assume that our experiences are common for everyone or everyplace. Neither Helen nor I had been in the Florida Panhandle. Our experience in Florida had been almost exclusively on the east coast and the area around Orlando. Jacksonville was the extent of our north Florida experience. We expected the Panhandle to be flat like all of the Florida we knew. What a surprise was in store for us! Starting in Pensacola we encountered hilly roads for the first time since we raced up the hill north of Waco, Texas.

178

These are some serious hills when you are going over them on a bicycle. Our Adventure Cycling Southern Tier Route Map had warned us that there were hills in the Panhandle, but they still caught us by surprise. We had plenty of opportunity to race up them and then to feel like we were flying down the other side. The 2424 miles we had ridden before Florida had gotten us into good condition. The hills were challenging, but we overcame them all.

We had lunch one afternoon in a pizza parlor in downtown Tallahassee. The young woman waiting on us had time to chat, since no one else was having pizza at that time. When I mentioned the hills, she told us in school in Tallahassee she had been taught the hills were the southern end of the Appalachian Mountains. I believe her teacher had it right.

Generally, highway 90 was good for cycling. However, trucks hauling timber made up for the lack of traffic. Tree farms appeared to be the primary agriculture. I was told trees are 14 years old when they are usually harvested, and most of them are used for pulp to make paper. These tree farms are often very large with sections being harvested each year.

The trucks hauling the long tree trunks were dirty spreading mud and tree bark all along the road. The drivers seemed to be more aggressive than those driving the big rigs on the interstates. The big rigs were more streamlined, and didn't cause a lot of wind turbulence when they passed. There was nothing streamlined about the logging trucks. They not only didn't move to the left to give us plenty of room, their turbulence made it hard to keep the bike under control. The

179

good thing was they made a lot of noise. We always had a warning, and could take evasive action when one was approaching.

A Sit-down Strike

After passing through Pensacola, traffic did start to pick up. We stopped in Milton for our first night after Perdido Key. The next morning at 4:00 a.m. we walked over to the Waffle House for breakfast before hitting the road. This was a Sunday morning. While we were getting our waffles, a car load of loud and obviously drunk people came in. They had been partying all Saturday night. Probably had decided they needed coffee so they could be wide awake drunks.

We finished our breakfast, went back to the motel for our bikes, and started the day's ride at 4:30. It was still very dark. I didn't like riding in the dark. Helen evidently had better night vision than I. We had little battery powered flashlights attached to our handlebars as headlights. We also had little flashing red lights on the back of our luggage racks. The routine was for Helen to lead the way, and for me to follow, complaining constantly until the sun came up.

There was a reason for the early start. We were getting into the "rainy season" and most afternoons there were thunderstorms. The one in Orange Beach, Alabama, had been an unusual morning storm. Helen's reasoning was good. I just couldn't see well enough in the dark to ever feel safe. I think the cataracts in my eyes were the cause of the crystal effect from

180

oncoming headlights that blinded me. All I could do was watch the little red light flashing on Helen's rear rack, and pray.

The morning we were leaving Milton, I was not only concerned about not being able to see, but also sharing the road with drunk drivers. As we pulled past the Waffle House, the drunks came stumbling out, and noisily got in their car. We were on the highway when they pulled out from the Waffle House, and started toward us. I insisted that Helen ride into the parking lot of the shops beside the road. Not wanting to be spotted, we got as close to the buildings as possible. My fear was they would think hitting bike riders was a fun sport. We stood by the bikes as they finally wove down the road, and out of sight.

Continuing on our way east out of Milton, we found ourselves in a construction zone. The road was being resurfaced, and evidently a new lane was being added on the right. To prepare for the new lane, any shoulder that might have been beside the road had been dug out. There seemed to be a drop-off of at least a foot at the right edge of the highway. It was dark, so I'm not sure how deep the drop-off really was. Then to make the situation worse, an old two-lane bridge was being replaced. There was no place to ride but in the one lane going east. If a car had approached at that time, I was sure we would be hit. This was another *chased by a pack of dogs* kind of bridge with the added excitement of not being able to see where I was going.

The construction continued on the east side of the bridge. Needless to say, I was not enjoying this wild ride. Ahead I saw lights from a gas station. When we got to the lighted station, I announced to Helen that I was stopping. We pulled in. I parked my bike, got off, walked over to a bench, sat down, crossed my arms, and announced that it was not safe for us to continue, and I was staying here until the sunrise when I could see the road I was riding on.

Helen was beside herself. We were missing the best part of the day for riding. If we got into storms later it would be my fault. She had other words and thoughts as she paced in front of me like a caged animal. I was unmoved. Announcing I was on strike; I was willing to sit there with my arms crossed until the sun came up. Helen kept pacing and muttering, and I sat looking straight ahead trying to ignore her.

After ten minutes, a pick-up truck came down the road from the east on the road we would be taking. It pulled into the station, and the men got out going in for coffee. Helen approached and asked them how far up the road the construction lasted. They told her that the construction ended right where we were. The road was in great shape all the way to DeFuniak Springs, our destination for the day. I meekly stood up, got on my bike, and got in line behind Helen. My strike was over. The rest of the day was actually one of the best rides on the whole adventure.

Tallahassee

We timed our arrival in Tallahassee for after 9:00 a.m. so as to avoid rush hour. It did avoid rush hour, but I suspect there was no rush hour at all that day. Florida State University was not in session, and neither was the Florida State Legislature.

Our home for the night was a high-rise Holiday Inn within walking distance of the capitol. This meant we had to walk the bikes through the lobby and onto the elevator to get to our room. Because business seemed to be slow the day we were there, no one seemed to mind our unorthodox method of arrival. We chalked this up to another unique experience.

We thoroughly enjoyed walking around Tallahassee. The downtown was clean. The old buildings had all been restored and the new ones fit in to make it a pleasant place for walking. There were few people in town that day, so we had the museum and restaurants much to ourselves.

The Old Capitol has been turned into a State History Museum. The current capitol is a high-rise office building towering behind the older building. In the early 1700's, a Spanish treasure fleet sank in a hurricane off the barrier island where we live. To this day, after Atlantic hurricanes people find Spanish coins and other treasure on our island's beach. A part of everything found goes to the state, and is housed in the museum we toured. I wanted to check it out to see if in fact the treasure was there, and it was.

Other items of interest in the museum explained how when Florida Territory petitioned to become a state, because they were going to be a slave state, they had to wait for another territory that was not going to be a slave state. It happened that Iowa was the next to petition for admission as a non-slave state. Florida and Iowa were paired by the U. S. Congress to enter together. However, there was something in the Congressional act that Iowa didn't like, so they refused to be admitted with Florida, and became a state a year later.

When Florida became a territory, the only two towns were Pensacola and St. Augustine. The territorial legislature alternated their annual sessions between these two towns. The legislators from Pensacola complained about having to go all the way to St. Augustine when they met there, and the next year the legislators from St. Augustine complained. It was decided to put the permanent capital exactly between the two. Surveyors determined Tallahassee to be the spot. That's why the Florida capital is up in the Panhandle

The large trees lining the streets with the wispy Spanish moss make Tallahassee a charming Southern city. The people were friendly and took pride in their hometown. They were eager to let us know the locations of the prettiest streets with the canopy of trees and moss giving one the sensation of riding through a tunnel. We appreciated getting directions to these streets, but were trying at this stage of our adventure to keep the bikes pointed east, so we put off the canopy experience side trips for the next time we ride through town.

Early the next morning I was following Helen's flashing red lights out of Tallahassee. We both agreed it had been one of the nicest places we had visited. This was definitely on our list of *must visit again cities*.

The Old Florida State Capitol

Greenville

The morning we left Tallahassee, we rode into the little town of Greenville looking for where we'd get breakfast. As we rode around the town, we both commented on how this place seemed different, and not in a good way. The streets in the downtown business district were deserted and dirty. The whole town seemed dead.

Finally, we located a person who pointed us in the direction of a café where we could get breakfast. There certainly was no Waffle House in Greenville.

We found the café, and were surprised when we noticed the windows all had iron bars over them. The door was also

185

covered with an iron grate. Several other buildings in town had similar decorations, but we hadn't expected them on the café. We had not seen this in any other town on our entire cross-continent ride.

Securing our bikes in front of the I where we'd be able to observe them from inside, we entered and found a table by the window. A waiter came over with a menu and a welcome.

As we were ordering, our attention was attracted to a commotion in front of the building. There were several well dressed men and women with a ribbon forming up in front of the café by our bikes. A photographer was directing everyone as to where to stand. They then cut the ribbon, and came in to greet us at our table.

We just happened to come to Greenville at the time the town was celebrating the reopening of the café under a new owner. We might have been the first customers. Besides the owner and the photographer, we were introduced to the mayor and city council. They let us know how happy they were to have tourists visiting there town. (I don't think it happens often.) They were very curious about our having arrived by bicycle, and didn't believe me when I told them we traveled by bikes because we couldn't afford the high priced gasoline. They all had the photographer take their picture with us. When our food arrived, they excused themselves, and left us to our breakfast.

One councilwoman didn't leave but got a cup of coffee, and came over and sat down. She was determined to tell us what a nice town Greenville is. We were both struck by how she was stressing that whatever we had heard about Greenville, it really was a nice, safe place. Until we arrived, we had never heard of Greenville. Her stressing *nice* and *safe* seemed a little unusual, but we just went on eating and being good listeners.

After breakfast, we thanked the councilwoman for her kind welcome, and for sharing the information about Greenville. We all said our good-byes, and we pedaled on east out of town. As we rode we were puzzled by our experience. It was truly a "what was that all about" moment.

Greenville, Florida

When we stopped that night in Madison, we asked the person at the motel if something had happened in Greenville recently. His eyes got big as he asked, "Did you stop in Greenville?" We told him we had had breakfast there. He explained that Greenville had been in the news a lot. It seems that two young men had broken into an old man's house. They

187

had robbed and brutally beaten him. I don't remember all the details, but he might have been murdered. Greenville had a reputation in the area as a tough place, and this incident had sealed the deal.

Evidently, the councilwoman had assumed we knew about the incident from the news. Her trying to convince us the town was a nice, safe place was her attempt to make-up for the town's bad reputation. Helen and I agreed that Greenville was not on our list of must visit again cities. However, the town did have a pretty, picturesque pond covered with lily pads.

Road Kill

Traveling along a highway at 13 miles per hour, you see and smell things you miss when inside a car traveling at the speed limit. I found the shoulder of roads in some parts of the country to be littered with parts off cars and trucks. There were so many wheel lug nuts lying loose on the shoulder of the roads I had to wonder how any wheels were staying attached. It is important to stay alert on a bicycle as you don't want to run over things that you wouldn't even notice in the car.

The road kill was always of interest. Most of it was on the shoulder like the lug nuts. Sometimes I would smell it, and have to look in the ditch to see what it was. Other times the sight and smell was enough to make me speed up to get out of smelling range. I'd hate to think how many poor animals are killed every day in this country as they try to cross highways.

188

The most common road kill seemed to be snakes. This was especially true in the west. The paved roads hold the heat longer than the desert sand. As the sun sets, snakes are drawn to the heat and slither up on the road to take advantage of the last heat of the day. The cars that flatten them probably don't even feel a bump as they roar down the road.

We observed plenty of raccoons and opossums. Some of them were already being a meal for vultures when we passed. These were the most stinky road kill. Of course a skunk would take the stinky prize, but I don't recall experiencing one on this trip.

Occasionally we saw deer. I always figured that for every dead deer, someone had a car in the body repair shop. These animals were large enough to do serious damage to any vehicle.

The saddest were the dogs and cats that had been someone's pets. Thankfully, we didn't see many of them, but in places where we were chased by dogs, you know that some also chase cars. None of them seemed to be afraid to get in the street and on the road.

The most spectacular road kill was the armadillo. This insect eating animal's body is covered with bony plates. When it is hit by a vehicle, the armadillo looks like it explodes. It isn't a neat piece of road kill. It is squished like the snake and the armor is scattered for a distance around the dead and smelly animal. I don't think even the vultures find anything good about this road kill. I was so impressed with these animals that I had to take a picture of one. It's not a pretty sight.

189

Armadillo road kill

Suwannee River

The Suwannee River carries water from the Okefenokee Swamp in Georgia through Florida to the Gulf of Mexico. When we crossed the Suwannee River, we were no longer in the panhandle of Florida.

This river has been made famous by the Stephen Foster song, *Way down upon the Swannee River.* Foster modified the name so it would have just two syllables for his song. Most people seem to have adopted Foster's two syllables; although you will still hear some Floridians pronounce it correctly.

Crossing the river, it looked different than any river we had crossed. This part of Florida sits on limestone, so the banks of the river are limestone rather than the more usual mud. It was very picturesque.

190

The roads in the panhandle tend to run east and west. In the peninsula of Florida, the roads tend to run north and south. Shortly after crossing the Suwannee River, we again left the Adventure Cycling Southern Tier Route. Our goal was still to go east to St. Augustine and then south to home in Melbourne Beach.

Suwannee River

From experience, I knew there were few bike friendly east-west roads in the peninsula. Having given up our route maps for now, I had to find a route east to our goal. Continuing on the present course would take us to Jacksonville. I didn't want to take on another large city, especially not having a good route map to get around or through it. There was also the St. Johns River to contend with. This large river is one of the few in North America that flows north. Its source is on the mainland just to the west of our home. It flows north until emptying into

191

the Atlantic Ocean through Jacksonville. Very few bridges span this river.

Helen and I were pondering our difficulty finding a road east to St. Augustine when we stopped at a Rodeway Motel in Lake City. As we entered, the young man behind the counter was excited to have bike tourists as guests. He asked if we needed any maps. Someone from a bike club in Gainesville had just dropped off a box of maps with instructions to give them to any bikers that might be stopping over in Lake City. He was wondering what to do with them when we walked in the door. This was an obvious answer to prayer.

The new maps gave us the best bike route to Gainesville and from there east to Palatka where we could rejoin our Southern Tier Route for our last leg to St. Augustine. We were coming down the homestretch and now knew how to get to it.

Familiar Faces and Home

Our pastor, David Walkup, had been tracking our progress across the country on a map posted in the Memorial Building at the Chapel by the Sea. He and others in the church were intrigued by our adventure as we inched our way across his map.

David had expressed concern about our welfare and safety. He even had a friend who lives in Tallahassee call us when we were there; asking if there was anything we needed.

Jim and Martha Walkup, David's parents, live near Gainesville. When we arrived in that city, they contacted us, and we arranged to meet. Riding to lunch in their car was the first time we'd been in a vehicle since the day in Louisiana when we caught a ride to Covington after Helen's accident and my *run in* with the cop. We enjoyed meeting the Walkups, and not only had a nice lunch, but also had a tour of Gainesville and the University of Florida campus.

The following day, we had David and Teri, his wife, and their daughters, Marlee, Bethany, and Rebekah, stop to see us in Palatka. The family was on their way to North Carolina for the annual meeting of the General Synod of the Associate Reformed Presbyterian Church. These were the first familiar faces from Melbourne Beach we had seen since leaving there with our bikes in March. We enjoyed catching up on happenings in our little community along the beach.

The day we were riding from Gainesville to Palatka, I heard a "POP" below and behind me on the bike. The bike continued to ride as usual and I figured that I must have ridden over something with my rear wheel that made the sound. At out next rest stop, I took a look at my rear wheel, just to make sure, and saw that a spoke had broken.

A broken spoke can be a major problem. Often, when one spoke breaks more pressure is put on spokes opposite it, and you get two or three more that break. Without all the spokes, the wheel can lose its roundness, start to wobble, and rub on the brake pads. Making headway under those conditions would be difficult if not impossible.

While there were extra spokes in my panniers, I didn't have any experience replacing a broken one. The logical solution for what to do while in the middle of a ride is to take as much weight off the wheel as possible. A hundred pounds could be taken off if I traded rear panniers with Helen and also had her ride my bike. This we tried. Even though our bikes are identical, we each have them set-up to fit our riding position and body size. After being on my bike for a few minutes, Helen decided this wasn't going to work. It was scary for her to be riding with a different seat and handle bar position. Rather than risk another fall, we got back on our own bikes. Helen did keep the heavier panniers for the ride to Palatka, which went without incident.

At Palatka, while waiting for the Walkups to arrive, I traded rear wheels with Helen. The next day she rode on to St. Augustine with the broken spoke rear wheel. Helen even had a couple of *dog sprints* without any difficulty with what was now her broken spoke.

I have mentioned several milestones as we pedaled east. These included crossing the Continental Divide, passing 1000 and then 2000 miles, and crossing the Mississippi River. Without doubt, the greatest milestone was riding to the lighthouse in St. Augustine. At that instant it struck me that we had actually traveled across North America using our own leg power. Many other people have done this, and most of them have done it faster. I doubt that many of them have been retirees in their 60's that made it unsupported. It was a sensation of accomplishment I wish everyone could have in their lifetime.

It was June 11, 2001, when we rode into St. Augustine. Brad had dropped us off at Tecate Divide in California on

March 31. We arrived in St. Augustine on our seventy-third day. My bike computer had been keeping a record of our miles each day and I kept a running total. My entry for June 11 included a trip total of 2943.1 miles.

My cousin, Jill Wright, lives just north of St. Augustine in Jacksonville. Her family had been following my email journals as we traveled east. We wanted to have dinner together so they could help us celebrate our arrival at the East Coast. Jill and John, her husband, and their two boys, Benson and Patrick, made the trip down from Jacksonville. Jill had emailed that Benson used our travels as *show and tell* in his kindergarten class. After dinner, Benson really wanted to see our bikes. I think he was disappointed when they looked like bikes he sees people riding all the time. However, when I put the panniers on, he was excited. Now they looked the way he thought they should. He seemed much more interested in the bikes than the riders.

Benson's class was not the only one that had been getting reports on our travels. There were classes in several schools across the country traveling along with us. To make the trip more educational for these students, I tried to include history and geography information in many of the email reports.

St. Augustine lighthouse

While we were preparing for this adventure, I was often asked when I thought we'd be getting home. I would reply, "This is an adventure and adventures don't go on a schedule, but if you want a date, I expect to be home by the Fourth of July." When it became apparent we'd be arriving before the Fourth of July, Cynthia Margeson, a teacher at Arlington Traditional School, wrote to let me know her class was disappointed we were finishing early.

The day after our arrival in St. Augustine, my rear wheel went to a bike shop for a spoke repair. We still had 160 miles more to ride before getting home. I wasn't yet through with my bike. We took advantage of the repair day to be tourists in St. Augustine, one of our favorite cities.

This was only the second bike shop we had needed for repair. The first was in Waco, Texas. Helen had been having problems with her rear derailleur which is the mechanism for moving the chain to shift gears. All it takes is an Allen wrench, and I had one. Helen rejected my offer to make the adjustment. As I recall, her exact words were, "I want someone working on my bike who knows what he is doing." While this lack of confidence in her riding companion disappointed me, I did have to agree that she had made a good point. Adjusting a derailleur was not one of my skills.

We stopped in Daytona Beach on our way south for a night. In case anyone doubted we were at the ocean for the lighthouse photograph, the beach one is further proof we had made it as far east as was possible. The last three days we were riding south.

197

At Daytona Beach on June 13, 2001

The last night on the road was spent in an Econo Lodge on highway 1 in Cocoa. We had thought we might get a little further, but smoke from a brush fire somewhere to our west made riding and breathing at the same time a little difficult, so we called it a day after riding sixty-two miles.

We had gotten a few calls on our cell phone while on the road. In Cocoa, a friend, Mildred Sorrell, called to let us know there would be a little welcome home party for us when we rode past the Melbourne Beach Mobile Park on A1A. Her question was what time should she be expecting us? We weren't used to getting that kind of question. I finally said it would be after 8:00 a.m. That seemed to satisfy her and raised our curiosity as to what to expect. We had prepared to ride; we hadn't really

198

prepared to arrive home. That was going to be another adventure.

The next call after Mildred's was from Yhanique Whitely. She introduced herself as a reporter for *Florida Today* who was writing an article about our adventure for the paper. As she interviewed me on the phone, I was impressed by the good questions she was asking. She seemed to know quite a lot about our trip. I asked how she knew so much, and was surprised when she said she had been following us on the Owls60 website.

My initial response was how people must feel when they find their phone has been tapped. She had violated my privacy! When I had written my email journal, I was thinking it was going to family and friends. They were my audience. Now I found out people I didn't even know had been reading them. How dare she read my personal emails? The feeling of being violated didn't last long. I realized that when you are writing something, and it is being published on the internet, you have no control over who reads it. This was a lesson learned. One I've kept in mind as I've been writing about my *Travels with Helen*.

A little after 8:00 a.m. on June 15, 2001, Helen and I pedaled into the little town of Melbourne Beach and headed south on A1A for our home. A photographer from *Florida Today*, Michael Brown, met us and took some photos for the article being written by Ms. Whitely. Traveling past Spessard Holland golf course, we could see ahead to where there was a welcoming sign, and people waiting to see us in front of the mobile park. I must admit that as an emotional person, seeing these friends who had been following our progress since we left in March, and were now cheering us on to the finish line, really got to me. I had to stop to get my emotions under control before going on to where they were waiting. Michael took some photos, and we then pedaled down for an emotional greeting

We enjoyed sitting around the Sorrell's home eating cake and talking. More people kept stopping by, and it seemed that we could have stayed all day answering questions and greeting friends. One comment made by many was how healthy we looked. I got the impression they thought we would be all beat up and haggard looking. With the road rash healed, we were probably in about as good physical condition as we've ever been. I'm sure they all could see that I'd packed on a few pounds eating waffles and Grandma's Cookies in the convenience stores. You've probably noticed those pounds if you compare the photos from California to Florida.

Finally, Helen pulled me away from the party, reminding me we still had 10 miles to go before we were home. Riding down highway A1A took us back to when we rode here in training for the ride across the country. That seemed like a long time ago.

Evidently the Walkup family had gotten back home. Riding past Mullet Creek Road, the girls were waiting to give us their welcome. In another mile, we pulled into our driveway.

For those who are interested in statistics, the final total distance traveled was 3104.3 miles. Our average was 48.5 miles per day. We had taken seventy-seven days. Sixty-four of the days were riding and thirteen were resting. The longest day was eighty-one miles from Globe to Safford in Arizona. The shortest day was the nine miles when we relocated and got pinned down by a deluge going from Orange Beach, Alabama, to Perdido Key, Florida.

The adventure was over. We had reached our goal.

This was our first day on the road.

EPILOGUE

At Home in Melbourne Beach, Florida

In the days following our return home from riding bikes across North America, our differing personality types were much in evidence.

Helen is a *get the job done* type. Reaching the destination was her *job*. Getting home she could check off a goal she had set for herself many years ago. Now she was ready to move on. She hadn't been able to play golf since breaking her elbow when she fell on a training ride back in December of 2000. Her first thought upon arriving home was wondering if she could still hit the golf ball. It didn't take her long to get back to the course to find out.

For several days after our arrival, I, on the other hand, was feeling depressed. My focus since committing to the bike ride in January of 2000 had been preparing for the long ride, and then executing it. Many days had been spent researching routes and equipment. I'm sure I made more than a hundred *to do* lists. Every day I was working on something related to the trip.

The daily routine while on the road always included a challenge and a mystery. There was something unknown about each day. Leaving in the morning, following Helen's flashing red light, complaining all the time, had become my natural routine. Every day was spent on a road I'd never seen, and ended in a totally unfamiliar place. You could say I was into the journey, and Helen was into the destination.

I have read where many mountain climbers after scaling a challenging peak have feelings of depression similar to what I was experiencing. These climbers were more into the challenge of the climb than the summit experience. I hadn't thought much about it when I read about the climbers, but at home in Melbourne Beach, I could identify with them. Thinking back to when I played football, I recalled that I was often a little depressed after a game, not because we had lost (we usually won), but because I liked playing the game so much I was disappointed when it ended.

Life was going on, and I needed to be in it. I couldn't sit around and mope for long. Since I was still taking up space above ground, I knew the Lord wasn't done with me. The Lord's book of life doesn't have any blank pages.

A few weeks before we had traveled to California in March, Helen and I talked with John Mariner, the Executive Director of World Witness, about short-term mission opportunities for retirees. He had suggested we call him when we got home, and we'd plan a trip to Mexico to check out the possibility of our starting an English program for the students in the seminary in Tampico.

A few days after arriving home, I gave John a call to let him know we were ready to move on to the trip to Mexico. We set the date for early September. Pastor David, and friends, Larry and Sherry Sietsma, were also on board for the Mexican *exploratory mission* trip.

While we were meeting at the seminary in Mexico with World Witness missionaries and Mexican pastors, we received a formal invitation from the seminary administrators to start the English program. We accepted the invitation, and committed to getting the program started as well as being the first teachers. I thought we were making a commitment for six weeks. As I write this, it is ten years later. Our work in Mexico continues. While we are no longer teaching at the seminary, the Lord led us in a direction we had not expected. I'm still traveling with Helen, and following her now to this foreign country and people we love.

In 1996 when we retired, there was no way I could have predicted the adventures I would have traveling with Helen. Becoming a missionary in Mexico was totally unforeseen back then.

I have heard people say we should *live one day at a time*. Looking back over my life, and especially the time since I retired, I find that days are not discrete units. They are interconnected. There are consequences tomorrow for what I've done today. The days of life are more like the links of a chain. They are all connected, and together the chain is my life.

Decisions made on one day may not seem important, but when looking back along the chain I can see how that decision has impacted every link that follows. There are definitely links and decisions that are *life changing*. The long bike ride with Helen was definitely *life changing* in ways we didn't always realize until days or years later.

I'll never forget how terrified I was standing at the top of In-Ka-Pah Gorge on our second day riding, and how Helen's courage inspired and encouraged me to get through my fear.

Stopping in little desert towns in the Southwest, we talked with people who we never would have met if we had been traveling in a more conventional way. In Palo Verde, California, I thought I was with a movie star when the women made so much over Helen. These people could appreciate a white haired woman who had gotten to their little desert town by using her own muscles.

This long ride certainly got us out of our *comfort zone*. After spending time in the little, dusty places, going into a colonia in Mexico to work with very poor people didn't seem at all uncomfortable. Not only had we gotten out of our comfort zone, but the zone had been greatly expanded.

All across the country there were people who kept crossing our path at the very time we needed them. I think of Taylor in Phoenix who gave our bikes a tune up in a 7-11 parking lot, Carla who carried our panniers into New Mexico, the brothers and sisters in Christ who welcomed us for Easter in Globe, Rick in Anson who had the eye doctor information, and the EMTs in the ambulance that was just a couple of minutes behind us on Interstate 12 when Helen fell. Looking back along this part of my life chain, it is obvious the Lord was being faithful to His promise to be with us, and to protect us. He has a plan that is yet being revealed as we progress further along the chain of life.

The best part of *Taking the Long Way Home,* and what I called *Travels with Helen* was Helen. We had been married

206

thirty-five years when we took this ride. I have always thought of her as my teammate as well as my wife. Her courage on this ride was truly inspirational. How she shook off falls and kept on going made the old Timex watch commercials seem tame. I will never forget lying by the road after I knocked her off the bike, and watching her scold the *bad dog,* and thinking I was in good hands traveling with this alpha female.

Helen has no sense of direction. Every morning, we'd go out to the dark road, and I'd point her toward the east. She would start pedaling with me following her red flashing tail light, and I knew she had no clue where she was going. Helen's confidence and courage led us down the dark roads, and each day we watched the sunrise together as our team inched its way east.

The story of the long bike ride is now over. Life doesn't stand still, and there is a story in every day just waiting to be told. How to share some of those stories is my next challenge. Perhaps you will read more from me in the future. The last chapter of *Travels with Helen* has yet to be lived.

G. Frank Miller
August 24, 2012
Melbourne Beach, Florida

19035452R00112

Made in the USA
Charleston, SC
03 May 2013